WILD EDIBLE
MUSHROOMS

WILD EDIBLE
MUSHROOMS

TIPS AND RECIPES FOR EVERY
MUSHROOM HUNTER

HOPE H. MILLER

FALCONGUIDES

GUILFORD, CONNECTICUT
HELENA, MONTANA

AN IMPRINT OF GLOBE PEQUOT PRESS

FALCONGUIDES®

FalconGuides is an imprint of Globe Pequot Press.

Falcon, FalconGuides, and Outfit Your Mind are registered trademarks of Morris Book Publishing, LLC.

Photos by Dr. Orson K. Miller Jr. and Hope H. Miller

Text design: Sheryl Kober
Layout: Kirsten Livingston
Project editor: Gregory Hyman

Library of Congress Cataloging-in-Publication Data
Miller, Hope H., 1943-
    Wild edible mushrooms : tips and recipes for every mushroom hunter /
    Hope H. Miller.
        p. cm.
    ISBN 978-0-7627-7143-1 (pbk.)
    1. Mushrooms—North America. 2. Cooking (Mushrooms)—North
America.
    I. Title.
    QK617.M535 2011
    641.3'58—dc23

                                                                  2011019100

Printed in China
10 9 8 7 6 5 4 3 2 1

To my late husband, Orson Knapp Miller Jr. He was the love of my life, my friend, my mentor, and my own personal tutor. None of this could have been done without his influence, love, and patience. Also to our daughters, Andrea, Annelise, Ginny, and their children, Erin, Cory, Lindsy, Logan, and Brooke.

ACKNOWLEDGMENTS

I can never forget all the wonderful people who joined us in our searches for the elusive mushrooms. The graduate students who are spread all over the globe were special to both Orson and me. They are the future of the science and represent him so well. He was proud of them all. The many amateur mycologists were ready to drop everything at a moment's notice to go and look for a special fungus Orson needed. They were responsible for finding many new species to science. A special debt of gratitude is given to the late Leeds and Marie Bailey who worked tirelessly to record and find species at all the Forays of the Southern Idaho Mycological Association. Leeds and Marie even joined us for 2 months in Australia, working as our field assistants. Our colleagues from around the world have been an inspiration as well. We had the good fortune to visit many of them over the years and bring back fond memories of good times.

This manuscript would not have been completed in time without the expert help from Eddie Culver, a friend and computer guru.

I can highly recommend this kind of life to anyone. I feel privileged to have been part of a wonderful life with a wonderful person.

CONTENTS

Contents

INTRODUCTION

When asked to do this book, I remembered when I was first asked, on my forays around the country and the world, if I could recommend a few edible mushrooms for people to learn. I remember that the question seemed overwhelming when faced with tables of the different mushrooms that were collected. I was sure I would never be able to learn the ones good to eat. I was told, "Learn about five new ones each time and it won't be so hard." I took that advice, and it wasn't long before I, too, had a few favorites.

My late husband, Orson K. Miller Jr., was a professional botanist who focused on fungi. I was lucky. I had my own personal tutor. His was a profession of which I could be very much a part. Our children, Andy, Lise, and Ginny, also were a part of it. We traveled the country looking for elusive mushrooms. Soon the grandchildren were also a part of the entourage. It was a treasure hunt every time we packed a lunch and went out in the forests and the fields. Of course, Orson was out collecting not just for the table but also for botanical specimens. Sometimes it was hard to decide where our mushrooms were to go—to the Herbarium for future study or to the kitchen for dinner.

When we started to collect, dry, and preserve the edibles, I needed recipes. Every time we went to visit friends and colleagues, they wanted to show off their favorites. I am indebted to them for allowing me to use their recipes in my cookbook. Although *Hope's Mushroom Cookbook* is now out of print, many of the best recipes from that collection have been included in this book.

In the first part of this book, I cover the ways to collect and take care of your gastronomic finds. Next come passages on preservation and storage. Information about the North American Mycological Association (NAMA) is also included. Their Web page includes a list of all the mushroom clubs in North

America. It is important to find a group of mushroom hunters to help you get started, and you surely will be able to find one near you. At the back of this book, a short glossary of terms and a bibliography are also included.

Following the introduction is a key to the mushroom groups covered in the book and photos of each group. Then come photos and detailed descriptions of mushroom species found in the United States, covering their locations, habitats, and some common names by which they are known. Most of the mushrooms described here are edible. The few that should be avoided are clearly described so you can avoid confusing them with the edible ones.

Accompanying each mushroom description is the Latin name (genus, and species), followed by a proper name, indicating the name of the person who first described the species. If the name is in parentheses, the second name indicates a person who has more recently studied the fungus and categorized it in a new genus. An example is *Calvaria cyathiformis* (Bosc) Morgan. The genus name is always capitalized and the species is lowercase. This information will help anyone who wishes to engage in a more in-depth study of fungi.

Under the descriptions of the different species is information about where and at what time of year they can be found. "Widely distributed" means they can be found throughout the country. Many mushrooms are found only under certain plants, so it's helpful to have a local plant and tree field guide with you while looking for mushrooms.

The second part of this book details recipes for delicious appetizers, soups, salads, and hearty entrees that you can make for yourself and for your family with your gastronomical field finds. All of the mushrooms described in this book as edible and choice will be good in any of the recipes. Some recipes suggest a specific mushroom that I favor in a dish, but many other mushrooms will work just as well.

I hope this proves a handy guide to take into the field and to use to identify mushrooms, bring them home, and use them in dishes the whole family will enjoy. Learn about these mushrooms and then expand your base of knowledge.

Why Eat Mushrooms?
If you are a mushroom lover, you likely already know many of the reasons why mushrooms are a delicious and valuable food source. But if you have friends or family who need convincing, here are some reasons to eat wild mushrooms.

1. They are good for you. Mushrooms have very few calories. According to the American Mushroom Institute, mushrooms are a good source of folic acid, which is beneficial to pregnant women. They also contain vitamins A, C, and D; all the B complex vitamins (thiamine, riboflavin, niacin, pyridoxine, pantothenic acid, and biotin); calcium; phosphorus; iron; copper; manganese; and potassium. They are also 99 percent fat-free and low in sodium, and they have no cholesterol. Research on other benefits of mushrooms continues, and new information is discovered all the time.

2. They taste good. In fact, unlike the button mushrooms we find in grocery stores, wild mushrooms have a wide variety of flavors. Of course, many wild mushrooms are now being cultivated, are sold in farmers' markets and grocery stores, and are beloved by many.

3. Best of all, they are free for the taking. (Mushrooms purchased at the grocery store can be expensive.)

4. Hunting mushrooms is a wonderful way to get the whole family out on a trip to the forest for a treasure hunt. Children are the best hunters, since they are so close to the ground and are so inquisitive.

How to Collect Mushrooms

There are some simple rules for collecting mushrooms for the table or scientific study. Both require the same methods and tools.

First, you must have some container in which to collect them, such as a basket or a box. Next, you must have some way to keep each species separate from the others. You might use waxed paper and make packets for them, have paper bags for each collection, or use aluminum foil. If you plan to reuse the foil, you must wash it before reusing to avoid contaminating a wonderful edible fungus with a poisonous one. Never use plastic wrap, baggies, or bags for collecting. Plastic will encourage the growth of bacteria or mold, which you do not want infecting your choice edibles.

Take with you a knife, a tent stake, or a garden trowel to get all the way down under the mushroom. You must collect the bottom of the stalk, since sometimes the most important characteristics for identification are below ground level. Some mushrooms are buried deep in the ground, but don't worry about destroying the fungus plant. The mushroom plant (fine threads in the soil called mycelium) continues to grow even if the mushroom is picked. It is from these threads that mushrooms grow. The mushroom is like the apple on the tree and the spores are the seeds in the apple. The important thing is to avoid raking the ground and breaking up the fungus threads. That could destroy the plant.

You must keep the mushrooms cool until you get home. You might use an ice chest or a cool place in your car. Do not put them in the sun. When you get home, refrigerate them immediately. Mushrooms spoil easily and you can easily become sick from eating one that sat on the kitchen counter for too long.

Spore print color is important for the identification of some groups of fungi. Take white slips of paper with you when you collect. These should be used for spore prints. Make sure that you use the most mature specimens to get a spore print. Place the cap, gill- or pore-side down, on the white paper and put the mushroom and paper in the bottom of your packet. Very often when you get home you will already have a spore print, which you can compare with the spore print color descriptions provided in this guide. If no print is visible, leave the mushroom and paper overnight in a cool place. Mushrooms will not drop spores if they are too hot or too dry. A piece of damp paper towel in the packet may help the spores to leave a print.

It is good practice to cut the mushrooms down through the middle to reveal the cap and stalk tissue. This way the presence of small holes made by insect larvae can be seen and the insects cut out. If you cut a puffball from top to the bottom, you will be able to see that no form, or shape, of a mushroom is there. When young and edible, it should look like a block of cream cheese (see page 15). Do not eat if it has changed color or has the shape of a mushroom inside it. Some poisonous mushrooms grow surrounded by such tissue and look similar to a puffball. If the mushroom is poisonous, you will see the shape of a mushroom inside (see page 18). Morels should be cut from top to bottom to make sure they are hollow-stemmed. False morels, which I advise against eating, are usually stuffed with some kind of tissue. They will not be hollow.

The thrill of the mushroom hunt is not just about eating mushrooms, but also getting outside and collecting and identifying them. Children love to collect, but they must be told not to eat them until a parent verifies that they are edible and cooks them. As well, they should be instructed not to put their hands in their mouths after picking.

Mushroom Clubs

There are many, many local mushroom clubs that hold meetings all year long. Some have been in existence since the early 1900s. Many of these clubs belong to the North American Mycological Association (NAMA). This group holds an annual foray somewhere in North America, during which they collect mushrooms, give lectures, eat what is found, sell books, and just have fun. For information go to the Web site: www.namyco.org. Other clubs may not be affiliated with the North American Mycological Association but may still be useful to you. Check with your local outdoors clubs to find them.

A Note on Toxins

Since the focus of this book is edible wild mushrooms, I will not discuss the toxins found in some mushrooms in depth. There are many field guides and other books that cover this subject, and many can be found in the bibliography in the back of this book.

You may encounter some very poisonous mushrooms in the field. That is why you should go collecting with someone who is knowledgeable about wild mushrooms. There are many mushroom clubs in North America and around the world. If you have collected in another part of the United States, Europe, Asia, or the Southern Hemisphere, know that the look-alike here may not be the same species. That is why it is important to go with a local who can identify mushrooms. When you hear of someone who gets sick collecting away from home, it is usually the case that he has mistaken a species there for one he knew at home.

If you become ill, it is important to bring some of the mushrooms with you to the emergency room so that an expert can identify them. It will then be possible to identify the toxins and aid the physicians in treating you. Many times, more than one species may be in a collection. Remember to eat only one new variety of mushroom at a time so that it will be easier to identify which mushroom gave you trouble. Finally, do not eat any fungi that grow on eucalyptus. They will be toxic.

A few things to remember:

Do not eat raw morels.

Do not mix types of mushrooms you have not eaten before in your dish. If you do mix them and become ill, you won't know which one made you sick.

Always identify and clearly label your collections with mushroom name and date picked.

Reserve a few mushrooms to take to the doctor in case you experience a sensitivity to them.

If you become ill from eating a mushroom, get immediate medical attention. Take the remainder of the mushrooms you ate with you to be identified.

Preserving Mushrooms

Mushrooms respond well to all kinds of preservation. Here are some easy ways to preserve. (Note that all mushrooms should be cleaned before being preserved.)

Cleaning: You do not need to soak mushrooms in salt water before eating or preserving them. However, some of the teeth fungi have many tiny parts that may contain insects, and these should be soaked in salt water for 10 or 15 minutes to remove the bugs. Slice your mushrooms from the cap to the bottom of the stalk to see if there are any insects in them. If there are, just cut the affected part out and use the rest. Very often only one part will be infected. Use a wet paper towel to wipe the mushroom clean.

Canning: Follow the directions for your home canner or processor. All edible mushrooms are suitable for canning.

Drying: Use a commercial food dehydrator or make your own. All you need are some window-size screens (metal, not vinyl). Raise the screens on bricks or something else nonflammable. The shelves or screens can be stacked two or three high with the bricks in between. Arrange the mushrooms to be dried on the screens so that some air will be able to pass through the mushrooms. Wrap the outside of your dryer with canvas and place a hot plate set on low heat underneath. Leave about 2 inches between the dryer and the floor so warm air can enter and rise through the mushrooms. Make sure the mushrooms are thoroughly dry before storing. Don't try to dry them in the oven; you will cook them this way. You can also try drying in the microwave following directions for drying fruit or flowers. Consult the manual for your microwave to see how long it will take to dry them. Before the invention of microwaves, people strung mushrooms on heavy thread and hung them over the wood stove. It works, except in humid climates. You should clean the mushrooms before drying so that you can crumble them before reconstituting if you need finely chopped mushrooms in your recipe. When you reconstitute the mushrooms, save the liquid for later use. Soak the mushrooms in warm water until soft to reconstitute them. If you are going to use them in soup, they may be dropped into the soup pot dry.

Freezing: Mushrooms should be sliced ⅛ to ¼ inch thick for quick freezing and placed on a cookie sheet. When they are frozen, place them in a plastic food storage bag or a container, label, and date. Use the oldest mushrooms first. When cooking, do not thaw them. Place the frozen mushrooms in a frying pan with hot oil. Cook for 30 seconds. If you want to add butter or herb butter, after 25 seconds add the butter and cook for the last 5 seconds. Remove them from heat and they will continue to cook. Then add them to your dish. They will taste as if fresh.

Special tips: Mushroom cubes may be made for future use. When rehydrating or cooking mushrooms, save the liquid. Strain it and put it into labeled ice cube trays. Use the cubes in soups, sauces, and even in omelets for added flavor.

Enjoy!

PARTS OF THE MUSHROOM

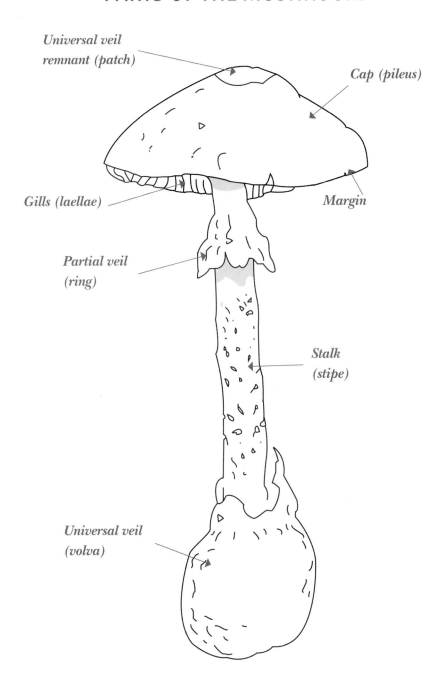

Universal veil remnant (patch)

Cap (pileus)

Gills (laellae)

Margin

Partial veil (ring)

Stalk (stipe)

Universal veil (volva)

Key to the Major Groups of Fungi Included in This Book

To use this key, compare the mushroom you have found with the pictures (page xx) identifying different types of mushroom. When you see one that is similar to your find, note the type (i.e., morel, false morel, puffball, or with a cap with pores).

Go to the key below and compare your find with the first two statements, each preceded by the number 1. Proceed to the number 2 or 5 statements, depending on which number 1 statement matches your find. Work down the key, and it will send you to a page and section where you should find a number of mushrooms in your group.

Note that there are thousands of mushrooms in the world and only forty edible ones are described in this book, along with three very poisonous ones.

1. Fruiting body a morel or false morel, puffball, or with a cap with pores --- **2**
1. Fruiting body with a cap with ridges, teeth, or gills --------------------- **5**
    2. Fruiting body with an oval or pine-cone-shaped top composed of distinct ridges and and pits, on a hollow, central stalk ------- **True Morels, page 2**
    2. Fruiting body with an oval to irregular or saddle-shaped top composed of a wrinkled to nearly smooth surface, on a central stalk, usually with soft tissue inside --------- **False Morels, page 8**
    2. Not as above --- **3**
3. Fruiting body fleshy and filled with a powdery spore mass when mature, round, oval, to pear-shaped with or without a pore at the top --------------------------**Puffballs, page 11, or Earth Balls, page 17**

True Morels

False Morels

Puffballs

Earth Balls

Boletes

Polypores

Teeth Fungi

Chanterelles

Agarics

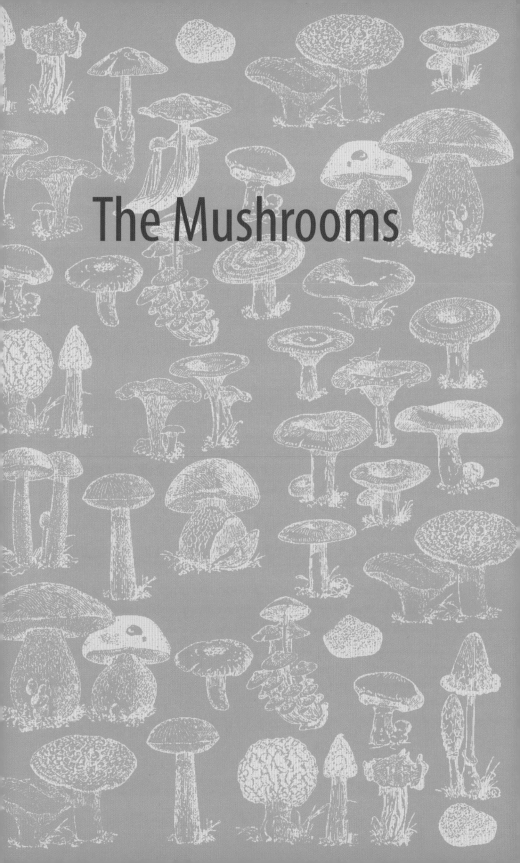

The Mushrooms

True Morels

Spring brings out morel hunters around the world, as the morels are the first fungi to come out each year. Those who want a great meal feel comfortable hunting morels since they are so distinctive. Those who will not hunt for anything else will be the first ones to go hunting for them in the spring. Morels are not easy to spot in forests and meadows. They are found in the East along streams, where old apple orchards grow, where elm trees are dying, and on east-facing slopes under oaks, pines, and mayapples. In the Northwest they are found the year or two years after forest fires. Central parts of North America host morels along streambeds and in tall grass prairies. In other words, they are found in many places. The important thing is to remember where you found them last year, as they will return for many seasons.

When is spring? It occurs at different times depending where you are. Fruiting generally starts in March in the Deep South; early April in Georgia and South Carolina; and late April through May in Virginia, Pennsylvania, New York, and throughout New England. Middle America usually has its best collecting in May or early June. The Canadians enjoy morels in June at low elevations but on into July at higher elevations.

Morels can be found at high elevation as late as late July to early August. The Rocky Mountain morels are primarily found in open parklike stands of Ponderosa pine and Engelmann spruce in May, but often at higher elevations in June and early July. Moisture is vital. As the forests dry out, the morels leave. Morels also seem to be more abundant where limestone occurs or on chalky (calcareous) soils.

This book includes a number of true morels but a general description will be given for most of them. This is because new information has revealed that North America's species are different from those found in Europe and Asia. The original names

2

came from Europe, but DNA studies have indicated that it will be necessary to give new names to the North American species. But to the person wishing to eat morels, the names are not important. All the true morels are good to eat as long as you personally do not have a sensitivity to certain ones. Try a little at a time if it's your first time eating morels. Do not eat false morels (page 8). Never eat morels raw.

Morchella esculenta Pers.: St.-Amans   edible and choice
Yellow Morel

Fruiting body 8–22 cm tall.

Cap 4–12 cm long, 3–12 cm wide, oval to conical or pinecone-shaped, with ridges and pits, irregularly arranged, yellow-brown to caramel brown, attached directly to the stalk.

Flesh brittle, interior hollow.

Stalk 3–11 cm high, 1.5–5.5 cm wide, nearly equal, with minute hairs, dull white to pinkish buff, hollow, often enlarged at base.

Odor none.

Taste mild.

Spore color buff to orange-buff.

Habit and distribution: Single, several, or gregarious on ground in a wide variety of habitats. Widely distributed. Fruiting in early spring to early summer.

Morchella crassipes Fr.   edible and choice
Thick-Footed Morel

Fruiting body 16–23 cm tall.

Cap up to16 cm tall, 9 cm wide.

Stalk up to 6 cm in diameter. The rest of the description is the same as *Morchella esculenta*.

Habit and distribution: Grows in dense grass communities and fruits a little later than other morels.

Morchella elata Fr.

edible and choice

Black Morel

Fruiting body 5–25 cm tall.

Cap 3–11 cm high, 3–8 cm wide, conical to rounded with elongated, longitudinally arranged ridges and pits, brown at first but soon with black to black-brown ridges and dark brown pits.

Flesh brittle, interior hollow.

Stalk 4–13 cm high, 2.5–7.0 cm wide, smooth to irregularly fluted and gnarled, roughened, surface white.

Odor pleasant.

Taste mild.

Spore color cream to light buff.

Habit and distribution: Single, several, or gregarious on ground under or near conifers. Widely distributed. Fruiting in early spring.

Comments: Also known as *Morchella angusticeps* Peck and *M. conica* Pers. It is most often conical with radially arranged pits, but in western North America, it is often ovoid to rounded and robust, but still has the typical black-brown ridges. It fruits in spring. It is one of my favorites and I dry it for future use.

Morchella deliciosa Fr.
White Morel

edible and choice

Fruiting body 2–11 cm tall.

Cap 2.0–4.5 cm high, 1.5–3.5 cm wide, broadly conic, rounded, with irregular white ridges and brown pits.

Flesh brittle, interior hollow.

Stalk 2.5–6.0 cm long, 0.9–3.0 cm wide, smooth, fluted or folded, hollow, dull white to cream.

Odor pleasant.

Taste mild and pleasant.

Spore color cream.

Habit and distribution: Single or several on the ground under dying elm trees, mulch beds, and humus in a variety of habitats. Widely distributed. Fruiting in the early spring and even in winter along the California coast.

Comments: The white morel is smaller than the yellow or black morel. It is not found in conifer habitats but shows up in Canada in late July.

Morchella semilibera (DC.:Fr.) Lév.   edible and choice
The Half-Free Morel

Fruiting body 2.5–20.0 cm tall.

Cap 2–4 cm high, 2.0–3.5 cm wide, conic to rounded with elongated longitudinally arranged brown ridges and pits, hanging skirt-like, flaring in age, partially attached halfway to the top of the stalk.

Flesh brittle, interior hollow.

Stalk 2–10 cm long,1–3 cm wide, equal, white to yellowish with fine granular material on the surface.

Odor pleasant.

Taste mild.

Spore color yellow.

Habit and distribution: Single to several on the ground in sandy soil under oak and beech, or along streams under cottonwoods and willows. Widely distributed. Fruiting a bit earlier than the other morels.

Comments: The half-free morel is the smallest of the morels, usually 4–10 cm tall. In Virginia, for instance, the best way to collect them is to stand at the base of a south-facing slope in oak forests and look up. The leaves cover the mushrooms and so it is easier to see them from below. This is true whenever they are found on hillsides. The tall slender stalks will stand out among the oak leaves. They are found throughout the United States.

False Morels

I have included the following false morels because many people have conflicting ideas about their identification and toxicity. Most notably, false morels have a stuffed or solid stalk. True morels have a hollow stalk.

Many people have eaten the snow morel in Pacific Northwest. In fact both my husband and I have eaten it in the past. New and extensive research on the toxins found in false morels, however, convinced us to stop eating them. Some people have suddenly become very ill after having eaten them for years. Some people who have cooked them but not eaten them have also become ill. The vapors from cooking have been considered the culprit.

There is also a look-alike for *Gyromitra montana* (found in Canada) that is quite poisonous. It is possible that this look-alike is extending its range to the northern United States. It is in your best interest to leave *Gyromitra montana* and its look-alike alone.

If you ever get ill after eating any mushroom, go for help and take a sample from your collection with you to the emergency room. Your physician will be better able to assess your condition and will be able to identify the mushroom and then inform the public, if necessary. Never eat more than a few bites the first time you try a new species. You must always be cautious about the potential for a food allergy. Do not combine more than one new species at a time: If you get ill, it will be difficult to tell which mushroom was the cause.

Gyromitra esculenta (Pers.:Fr.) Fr.   **poisonous**
Common False Morel

Fruiting body 5–18 cm tall.

Cap 5–6 cm high, 6–9 cm wide, convoluted and lobed, yellow-brown young, becoming brown to blackish brown at maturity, attached at apex.

Flesh brittle, stalk at first stuffed with white cottony mycelium (tissue), which collapses in age, becoming hollow.

Stalk 5–14 cm high, 1–3 cm wide, densely matted with wooly hairs, fluted to irregular in shape, cream with shades of brown to red-brown.

Odor mild.

Taste mild.

Spore color cream.

Habit and distribution: Single, several, or gregarious, sometimes in clusters, on the ground, under conifers. Found in western North America. Fruiting in spring, usually late April to late June, depending on elevation.

Comments: This species has toxins that are driven off by cooking. Inhaling the steam may cause the cook to be toxified. The toxins can cause vomiting, abdominal cramps, diarrhea, and other unpleasant symptoms. Rats fed this fungus in studies developed large carcinomas. Some people have eaten it without immediate effect but after a few years become toxified. I strongly recommend against eating this species. *Gyromitra ambigua* (P. Karst.) Harmaja is very similar but has smaller spores and is also poisonous. It has been found in parts of the United States and is distributed north into western Canada.

Gyromitra montana Harmaja   **nonpoisonous**
Snow Morel

Fruiting body 9–20 cm tall.

Cap 4–7 cm high, 3–7 cm wide, with deep lobes and convolutions, yellow-brown to caramel brown until very old, then dark brown, attached at apex but margin closely clasps the stalk.

Flesh firm but brittle, stalk stuffed with cottony white mycelium which collapses in age.

Stalk 6–16 cm high, 3.0–6.5 cm wide, longitudinally fluted or ribbed, minutely felted, white remaining so with slight brown stains where handled.

Odor mild.

Taste mild.

Spore color cream.

Habit and distribution: Single, but most often several fruiting just under or at the edge of or very near melting snowbanks, occasionally some distance away. Found in western North America. Fruiting in the spring, during the snow melt in May to early July (higher in the mountains).

Comments: *Gyromitra gigas* (Krombh.) Quél. has traditionally been the name given to this species. The European species have smaller spores than those in the United States.

Puffballs

There is rarely any time when puffballs are not fruiting some-where in North America. They fruit in forests, in fields, along hard-packed dirt roads, in mulch beds, and in your lawn. There are many good edibles in this group. Some people love them all and others are only interested in a few. The reason we find them in such diverse habitats is that they are decomposers; they thrive on all types of grass, plants, trees, mulch, and even toxic material.

After collecting them, puffballs should always be cut from the top to the place of attachment to the ground. The interior should be pure white throughout. It should look like you have cut through a block of cream cheese. The inside should *not* show the outline or shape of a mushroom. Fungi with this outline are the egg or button of a poisonous agaric. These can be fatal to eat and should be strictly avoided. Poison control centers find that many people mistake these buttons for puffballs. Each fruit-ing body should be examined in the same manner.

After verifying that your collection is in fact a puffball, keep it in the refrigerator. Do not leave puffballs on your kitchen counter before cooking; they can spoil even though they still look fresh. There are many good ways to prepare puffballs for the table; see Puffballs Parmesan (p. 66).

Calvatia gigantea (Batsch:Pers.) Lloyd   edible and choice
Giant Puffball

Fruiting body large, 20–35 cm high, 20–55 cm wide, nearly round, white to light gray to yellow in age, base with a thick root.

Outer skin smooth, felt-like.

Flesh white at first to olive-brown at maturity.

Sterile base lacking or very reduced.

Odor none when young, very unpleasant in age.

Taste mild and pleasant.

Spore color olive-brown in age.

Habit and distribution: Single to several together in wet areas near streams, in woods, or along edges of meadows. Widely distributed, rarely found in the Rocky Mountains, occasionally found in the Pacific Northwest. Fruiting in late summer and fall.

Comments: This fungus is found mostly in the East. See *Calvatia booniana* for the Western Giant Puffball. Both are delicious edibles. The largest known puffball was eighty pounds. Remember the location where you find one, because it will be there again the following year.

Calvatia booniana A. H. Sm.
Western Giant Puffball

edible and choice

Fruiting body large, 10–30 cm high, 20–60 cm wide, oval, depressed to flattened, dull white to light tan or buff, base with a small, thick, fibrous cord.

Outer skin sculptured, soon separating into large, flat scales.

Flesh white at first to olive-brown at maturity.

Sterile base lacking.

Spore color olive-brown at maturity.

Habit and distribution: Single or several on bare ground, in open pastures, grassy areas, near old corrals, often near or under sagebrush. Widely distributed in western North America. Fruiting in late spring, summer, and early fall.

Comments: This fungus is found nowhere else in the world. It has been collected and eaten since pioneer days. I find it equal in flavor to *C. gigantea.* I have fed fifty people from one of these puffballs.

Calvatia cyathiformis (Bosc) Morgan   edible and choice
Lilac Puffball

Fruiting body 9–20 cm high, 7–16 cm wide, nearly pear-shaped but with a thick base, white to light pinkish tan, brown in age.

Outer skin smooth, soon minutely cracked and sculptured over the top, smooth but wrinkled over the base and sides.

Flesh white, yellow to purple-brown in age.

Sterile base occupies the lower one-third of the fruiting body, chambered, white to dingy yellowish.

Odor pleasant.

Taste mild.

Spore color purple to deep purple-brown in age.

Habit and distribution: Scattered to numerous in old fields, grass, prairie, or desert communities, often following heavy rains. Widely distributed. Fruiting in summer and fall.

Comments: *Calvatia craniiformis* (Schwein.) Fr., the Brain Puffball, is very similar to *C. cyathiformis* except the flesh turns bright yellow to yellow-brown in age. Both these species are good edibles.

Calbovista subsculpta Morse edible

Fruiting body 6–12 cm high, 8–16 cm wide, globose or slightly depressed with a base often smooth to wrinkled but not warted, white when young.

Outer skin with slightly raised but not pointed warts, brownish to reddish hairs at the center of each wart.

Flesh firm and white, becoming red-brown to dark brown at maturity.

Sterile base occupies the lower one-fourth to one-third of the fruiting body, composed of minute chambers, dull white to slightly yellowish in age.

Odor none.

Taste pleasant.

Spore color yellowish.

Habit and distribution: Single, several, or gregarious on hard dry road beds, stock driveways near or under conifers. Found in western North America. Fruiting in late spring and summer.

Comments: This puffball is usually softball-size or sometimes larger but never with the pointed, pyramidal warts of *Calvatia sculpta* (Harkn.) Lloyd.

Lycoperdon perlatum Pers.   edible
Gemmed Puffball

Fruiting body 3–7 cm high, 3–6 cm wide, pear-shaped, dull whitish to light tan.

Outer skin densely covered with small, round, cone-shaped spines, which break off, leaving notice-able round spots.

Flesh white when young to olive-brown in age, sometimes tinted purplish at maturity.

Sterile base composed of large white chambers, discoloring to olive-brown.

Odor none.

Taste mild.

Spore color olive-brown.

Habit and distribution: Single, numerous to in clusters, in duff and humus under hardwoods and conifers. Widely distributed. Fruiting in summer and fall.

Comments: Lycoperdons are very commonly found in mulch beds. They are decomposers and will consume your wood chips. The flavor is not as good as that of the Calvatias; best when cooked in butter until very crisp.

Earth Balls

Earth balls have several features that are distinctly different from true puffballs. As they develop, their spores mature in chambers or locules. The flesh is white at first, but it quickly matures and becomes violet-gray to purple, flecked with white tissue. There is usually some color even in the young specimens. The outer skin is much thicker than that of most true puffballs. Another difference is that earth balls are mycorrhizal, or symbiotic, with many hosts, while true puffballs are decomposers.

Earth balls are poisonous and bitter tasting. They cause severe gastric upset and should be avoided. One student ate more than twenty Sclerodermas after being warned not to and was very ill for several days.

Scleroderma citrinum Pers.:Pers.   poisonous

Fruiting body 3–6 (up to 12) cm broad, globose when young, depressed at maturity.

Outer skin up to 2 mm thick, brown, covered with cracks that set off a pattern of raised warts that may have central, somewhat darker warts, extending almost to the base, in age splitting to reveal the spore mass.

Flesh very firm, briefly white, soon deep violet-gray to purple with small locules separated by fine white membranes, when mature black-brown and powdery.

Sterile base a slight broadening of the outer skin, white but bruising yellowish to faintly pink.

Odor none.

Taste bitter.

Spore color dark brown.

Habit and distribution: Single to several in sandy loam, under hardwoods and conifers. Widely distributed. Fruiting in spring and fall.

Comments: Also known as *Scleroderma aurantium* Pers., this species forms mycorrhizae with many different hosts. All Sclerodermas are poisonous and should be avoided.

Boletes

Boletes are fleshy mushrooms that have a cap, a central stalk, and pores on the underside of the cap. The pores are actually tubes usually 5–20 mm long. The spores are contained in these tubes and are forcibly discharged. The spore color is important for distinguishing among genera and species in the boletes. Boletes also have distinctive stains when cut or bruised. All boletes are mycorrhizal with specific trees (such as aspen, oaks, pines, or conifers), so it is important to identify the trees in the area. Some boletes are edible and choice (including the porcini of Italy), some are not poisonous but not tasty, and some are poisonous.

Boletus edulis Bull.:Fr.   edible and choice
King Bolete, Porcini, Cepe, Steinpilz, Penny Bun

Cap 8–37 cm broad, broadly convex, smooth but often uneven, dry, moist to slippery feeling, or slightly sticky when wet, yellow-brown becoming cinnamon-brown to red-brown with age.

Flesh firm, white, sometimes reddish just under the cap, unchanging when bruised.

Tubes 10–40 mm long, mouths small, 2–3 per mm, depressed just at the stalk, white at first, slowly yellow, yellowish olive to olive-brown in age.

Stalk 10–15 cm long, 2–6 cm wide, equal or with a bulbous base, whitish to yellow or yellow-brown, with fine white reticulations overall or nearly to the base, dry.

Partial veil absent.

Odor none.

Taste mild and pleasant.

Spore color olive-brown.

Habit and distribution: Solitary to gregarious under conifers and hardwoods. Widely distributed. Fruiting in spring, summer, and fall.

Comments: This is one of the most sought-after edible mushrooms in the world (along with morels). The shape of the stalk and color of the cap vary a great deal throughout North America. *Boletus barrowsii* A. H. Sm. is cream-colored with a pinkish hue. It is found under conifers in the southern part of western North America and occasionally found in the northern part of North America.

Boletus zelleri (Murrill) Murrill   edible and choice
Zeller's Bolete

Cap 4–12 cm broad, convex to plane in age, finely powdered at first, dry, deep brown, blackish brown to dark chestnut-brown.

Flesh firm, buff to yellow, slowly changing to blue when bruised (occasionally not changing).

Tubes 5–15 mm long, mouths large, 1–2 per mm, depressed at the stalk, yellow, olive-yellow in age.

Stalk 5–10 cm long, 1–3 cm wide, equal, red to brownish red, may be yellow at the base, smooth, dry.

Partial veil absent.

Odor none.

Taste mild.

Spore color olive-brown.

Habit and distribution: Several to gregarious under western conifers. Found in western North America. Fruiting in late summer and fall.

Comments: Mycorrhizal with conifers. I find it compares favorably with the King Bolete in taste.

Austroboletus betula (Schwein.) E. Horak edible
Birch Bolete

Cap 3–10 cm tall, convex, smooth, viscid, dark maroon-red to orange-red, or even yellow-orange.

Flesh orange-yellow, yellow, but sometimes tinted olive-brown.

Tubes 10–20 mm long, mouths large, 1 or more per mm, depressed just at the stalk, bright yellow becoming tinted olive, then olive-brown.

Stalk 10–27 cm long, 0.5–2.3 cm wide, equal, tall and thin, deeply reticulate, bright yellow becoming stained reddish over the lower half in age, with white mycelium at the base.

Partial veil absent.

Odor none.

Taste mild.

Spore color brown.

Habit and distribution: Several to numerous under mixed hardwoods and pine. Found in southeastern and southern North America. Fruiting in late summer and fall.

Comments: This bolete is mycorrhizal with pines and probably oaks and beech. *Boletellus russellii* (Frost) Gilb. looks similar, but has a dry, yellow-brown cap and a long, thin stalk with coarse, shaggy reticulations and is found in the eastern and southwestern United States.

22

Suillus cavipes (Opat.) A.H. Sm. & Thiers   edible
The Hollow Stem Suillus, Mock Oyster

Cap 3–12 cm broad, convex to broadly convex, plane, or with a low umbo in age, dense cinnamon-brown scales over the entire surface, tips often white, edge of cap with torn remains of the partial veil, dry.

Flesh soft, white to buff, not changing when bruised, stalk base hollow.

Tubes 3–6 mm long, mouths 0.5–1.0 mm wide when mature, decurrent, strongly radially aligned, bright yellow.

Stalk 3–9 cm long, 0.6–2.0 cm wide, enlarging somewhat at base, dry, yellow above the partial veil, below covered with scales same color as cap.

Partial veil white, fibrous, leaving a cinnamon-brown ring.

Odor none.

Taste mild.

Spore color olive-brown.

Habit and distribution: Often abundant under larch or tamarack. Widely distributed. Fruiting in late summer and fall, until late frost.

Comments: This species is easily identified by the hollow foot. It is highly desirable in mushroom casseroles.

Suillus luteus (Fr.) Gray   edible and good
Slippery Jack

Cap 4–17 cm broad, convex to broadly convex in age, smooth, viscid to glutinous, forming a layer that can be peeled off.

Flesh white to pale yellow.

Tubes 3–7 mm long, mouths 3 per mm, broadly attached to the stalk, radial in age, white at first to pale to deep yellow with a brownish tint in age.

Stalk 4–11 cm long, 1.0–2.5 cm wide, equal, yellow with pink to pinkish brown glandular dots above the partial veil, pale yellow to nearly white and glandular dotted below.

Partial veil white, membranous, persistent, with a purplish zone on the underside, gelatinous in humid weather.

Odor not distinctive.

Taste mild and pleasant.

Spore color dull cinnamon.

Habitat and distribution: Scattered to numerous wherever two- and three-needle pines are found, especially in Scotch pine and Austrian pine plantations. Found in the northern boreal forest or in colder mountainous regions. Fruiting from late summer until late fall.

Comments: This is an excellent edible with firm flesh. Remove the slimy layer from the cap and the pores before cooking. Europeans know this species from their home countries and look for it especially in Middle America.

Edible Polypores

Polypores are unique. They do not resemble any other group of fungi. The spores are discharged from the pores. They are mostly decomposers; some are parasites, and some are mycorrhizal. They are found on trees, on roots, and on the ground. Most of them are too leathery or hard to be good edibles; others have only a narrow edge of the cap that should be eaten. A few are delicious. Do not eat any polypore that grows on eucalyptus, because it will make you sick.

At the end of this section I include one species, *Sparassis crispa*, that is not really a polypore but grows in similar habitats, and for the scope of this book, fits here and nowhere else.

Laetiporus sulphureus

edible and choice

(Bull.:Fr.) Murrill

Sulphur Shelf, Chicken Polypore

Fruiting body 5–25 cm broad, shelf-like, with an overlapping series of orange-yellow caps.

Flesh firm, margin soft to tough near center, white to yellowish.

Tubes 3–4 mm long, pores 2–4 per mm, bright sulphur-yellow.

Stalk absent.

Odor mild.

Taste mild.

Spore color white.

Habit and distribution: Shelves on stumps, logs, or wounds on standing trees. Found in eastern North America. Fruiting in spring, summer, and fall.

Comments: Only the soft tissue on the edge of this polypore is edible. If you take too much, your whole dish will become bitter. If you leave the fruiting body in place after taking the soft part, a new one will grow back. The similar *Laetiporus conifericola* grows on conifers from California to Alaska. For other edible species, see descriptions in *North American Mushrooms*.

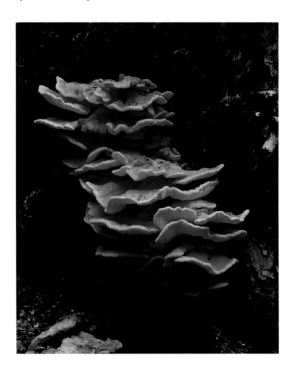

Laetiporus cincinnatus
(Morgan) Burds., Banik, & Volk

edible and choice

Fruiting bodies 45–60 cm in diameter, as a rosette, with numerous large caps up to 15 cm wide, 10 cm deep, 3 cm thick, orange-yellow.

Tubes 1–5 mm long, 2–4 per mm, nearly circular at first, becoming more angular in age, pale cream.

Stalk thick, centrally attached, bright salmon-orange.

Odor mild.

Taste mild.

Spore color white.

Habit and distribution: On soil from buried roots, near the base of large old hardwoods, but rarely on trunks or logs. Found throughout the eastern and midwestern United States, except along the Gulf Coast. Fruiting summer and fall.

Comments: This species is distinct from others in the genus in that it fruits as a rosette, on the ground from buried wood. It is a very good edible. Take only the soft, yellow edges. First found and described in Cincinnati, Ohio.

Grifola frondosa (Dicks.:Fr.) Gray   edible and choice
Hen of the Woods

Fruiting body large, up to 60 cm broad, composed of many overlapping caps 2–8 cm broad, hairless to minutely fibrillose, gray to gray-brown, dry.

Flesh firm, white.

Tubes 4–5 mm tall, 1–3 pores per mm, small, white to yellowish in age.

Stalk large, compound, short, white.

Odor mild.

Taste pleasant.

Spore color white.

Habit and distribution: Usually single on the ground from buried roots and wood, near but not on stumps and snags of oaks or other hardwoods. Found in eastern, southeastern, and midwestern North America, rarely in the Pacific Northwest. Fruiting in late summer and fall.

Comments: This is one of the truly delicious edibles. Its bulk makes it a prize find. The flavor is fairly strong and is excellent in soup or turkey stuffing or as the major component of a mushroom loaf.

Make note of the description of *Meripilus giganteus,* which is often confused with *Grifola frondosa.* It turns black when bruised and has a rather unpleasant odor and somewhat acid taste. I recommend avoiding it.

Albatrellus ovinus (Fr.) Murrill
Sheep Mushroom

edible and good

Fruiting body annual, with a central stalk.

Caps 4–15 cm broad, with minute hairs, dry, white, cream to light orange-brown.

Flesh firm, breakable, cream to buff, with a dark layer near pores.

Tubes 1–2 mm tall, 3–5 pores per mm, descending down the stalk, cream, pinkish to pinkish brown.

Stalk 3–8 cm long, 1–3 cm wide, central to slightly off-center, white, bruising light pinkish brown, dry.

Odor pleasant, even aromatic.

Taste mild.

Spore color white.

Habit and distribution: Single to several, on the ground under conifer forests, especially spruce and fir. Widely distributed. Fruiting in late summer and fall.

Comments: It has been eaten for years in the United States. Tastes vary—many enjoy it, but others are not so fond of this mushroom.

Sparassis crispa Wulfen:Fr.   edible and good
Cauliflower Fungus

Fruiting body in a rosette or cauliflower-like, 25–50 cm tall, 15–35 cm wide, white to yellowish, with many flattened branches with flattened tips.

Flesh firm, soft when young to somewhat tough in age.

Stalk large, 2–4 cm thick, central, deeply rooted.

Odor not distinctive.

Taste mild and pleasant.

Spore color white.

Habit and distribution: Single or occasionally several on the ground under conifers. Widely distributed. Fruiting in late summer and fall.

Comments: This is really not a polypore (it does not have pores), but it is smooth and for this book fits best here. This fungus will grow in the same place for successive years, so remember where you found it. Soak it in salt water to eliminate insects. It can also be frozen and will reconstitute very well.

Poisonous Polypores

These two species of polypore are here because many people mistake them for edible ones. Many people have become quite ill when eating these two species; some do not.

Meripilus giganteus (Fr.) P. Karst. **not recommended**
Giant Polypore

Fruiting body annual, large, 40–80 cm broad, brown or tinted gray often with a wavy white margin, smooth or with fine scales, dry.
Caps overlapping, brown or tinted gray.
Flesh firm, fibrous, white, often staining black when bruised.
Tubes 5–8 mm deep, 3–5 pores per mm, white, black when bruised or upon drying.
Stalk very short, stout, centrally attached to buried wood.
Odor unpleasant but not distinctive.
Taste mild but somewhat acrid.
Spore color white.
Habit and distribution: Single to several on the ground under hardwoods, especially oak and beech. Found in eastern North America. Reported from Idaho, but I have not seen it. It may have been transplanted with eastern hardwoods. Fruiting in late summer and fall.
Comments: The caps are larger than those of *Grifola frondosa,* which does not bruise black. Some people have eaten it, but most find it unpalatable. I do not recommend it.

Albatrellus confluens (Alb. & Schwein.:Fr.) Kotl. & Pouzar

Inedible

Fruiting body annual.

Caps 4–11 cm broad, often fused together, cream, buff, pinkish buff to light orange-brown in age, sometimes with blue tints, cracked especially in age, dry.

Flesh firm, but easily broken, white at first, cream to buff in age.

Tubes 2–5 mm tall, 3–5 pores per mm, pure white when young, straw-yellow or mustard-yellow in age, often extending down the stalk.

Stalk 2.5–6.5 cm high, 0.9–2.4 cm wide, central to slightly off-center, ovoid, robust and irregular, smooth, white to buff in age, sometimes orange-brown at base, dry.

Odor pleasant, even fragrant.

Taste mild.

Spore color white.

Habit and distribution: Single or with many fused stalks and fused caps on conifer duff, under a wide variety of conifers. Widely distributed. Fruiting in summer and fall.

Comments: This fungus may be almost entirely blue if it has been bruised. This species is very bitter or without flavor. I do not recommend it, as it needs to be vigorously boiled and even then has questionable flavor. It is sold in Scandinavia in the farmers' markets, despite its bitterness, and they will boil it before using.

Teeth Fungi

The genera of the teeth fungi are delineated by spore color. I cover three genera, *Hydnum* and *Hericium,* which have white spores, and *Sarcodon,* which has brown spores. Identifying teeth fungi by spore color is a more modern practice, and many older mushroom books do not use this method. All of the species described in this section are edible and choice. The first three grow on the ground and the last two on trees.

Hydnum repandum L.:Fr.   edible and choice

Cap 3–10 cm broad, convex, broadly convex in age, buff to orange or fading orange, margin wavy, smooth, dry.

Flesh thick, soft and brittle, light yellowish.

Spines 4–8 mm long, with various lengths intermixed, cream.

Stalk 2–8 cm long, 0.5–2.0 cm thick, solid, smooth, dry, white, sometimes with pale orange or buff tinges.

Odor none.

Taste delicious.

Spore color white.

Habit and distribution: Single to numerous, under hardwoods or conifers. Widely distributed. Fruiting summer and fall.

Comments: Also known as *Dentinum repandum,* this species is edible and delicious. It is found around the world and sought after by all who eat wild mushrooms.

Hydnum albidum Peck   edible and choice

Cap 1–7 cm broad, convex soon plane, white to creamy, felty, dry.

Flesh soft, white, light orange when cut or bruised.

Spines 4–7 mm long, white, extending down the stalk.

Stalk 2–5 cm long, 0.8–2.0 wide, smooth, white.

Odor none.

Taste mild.

Spore color white.

Habit and distribution: Single to several, under conifers and hardwoods. Widely distributed. Fruiting in summer and fall.

Comments: I have collected this species at the same time that I collected *Hydnum repandum*. They are equally good eating.

Sarcodon imbricatus (L.:Fr.) Karst.   edible and good

Cap 8–30 cm broad, convex with a depressed center, covered with coarse, raised brown scales, dry.

Flesh easily breaking but not soft, white to very light brown.

Spines 5–15 mm long, extending down the stalk, brown.

Stalk 4–10 cm long, 1.5–3.0 cm wide, enlarging toward the base, smooth, light brown, dry.

Odor none.

Taste somewhat bitter.

Spore color brown.

Habit and distribution: Single to several, under conifers or mixed conifers and hardwoods. Widely distributed. Fruiting in summer and fall.

Comments: The largest specimens I have found were in Alaska. A closely related species, *S. scabrosus,* is very bitter, has more red coloration, and has a bluish black stalk. Eating it is not recommended.

Hericium erinaceus (Bull.) Pers.
Lion's Mane

edible and choice

Fruiting body 5–41 cm broad, 5–24 cm wide, oval solid, white, dingy yellowish in age.
Flesh firm, somewhat spongy, white.
Spines up to 3.5 cm long, white, crowded below, attached to wood by a solid white cord.
Odor fungoid.
Taste mild and pleasant.
Spore color white.
Habit and distribution: Single, from wounds on hardwood tree trunks, often high up. Widely distributed. Fruiting in late summer and fall.
Comments: This is a very good edible. Mushroom growers cultivate this species for sale in specialty markets. Another good species is *H. erinaceus ssp. erinaceo-abietus* Burds, O. K. Mill. & Nakasone. It is similar in growth form, but it has small, very short, white spines, and it is frequently found in the southern and central United States. It fruits on decaying hardwood logs, limbs, and stumps.

    Soak *Hericium* species in water before preparing them for the table. This will bring out any insects that might be hiding among the spines. It is not a bad idea to parboil them for a few minutes to soften the flesh. These species are a good addition to casseroles when bulk is needed.

Hericium coralloides (Scop.) Pers.   edible and good
Coralloid Hericium

Fruiting body 10–30 cm broad, with many branches, pure white to yellowish in age.
Flesh fibrous, white.
Spines 5–15 mm long, hanging down all along the branches, which arise from the white fleshy central core.
Odor pleasant.
Taste good.
Spore color white.
Habit and distribution: Single, on sides of logs, stumps, and limbs of both hardwoods and conifers. Found throughout North America. Fruiting in late summer and fall.
Comments: Soak *Hericium* species in water before preparing them for the table. This will bring out any insects that might be hiding among the spines. It is not a bad idea to parboil them for a few minutes to soften the flesh. These species are a good addition to casseroles when bulk is needed.

Chanterelles

Chanterelles exhibit distinctive characters, allowing novices to quickly increase their lists of edibles. The general look of an edible chanterelle is that of a trumpet, almost always with a shallow or deeply depressed cap. Chanterelles have gill-like low ridges, are nearly smooth, and have white spores. One species, *Polyozellus multiplex*, is deep violet-black, grows in clumps, and has white spores.

These fungi are sold in farmers' markets around the world and are prized by many. The only chanterelles to be avoided are three species of *Gomphus* that are reported to cause gastro-intestinal upset in some people (see *North American Mushrooms* for descriptions of all three). One edible species of *Gomphus* is described here.

Cantharellus cibarius Fr.   edible and choice
Golden Chanterelle

Cap 3–17 cm broad, depressed with a recurved, wavy margin at first, to deeply depressed in center in age. Orange, orange-yellow to whitish yellow, sometimes tinted pink, smooth, dry.

Flesh firm, thick, light yellow.

Ridges blunt, gill-like, with veins between, often forked, extending down the stalk, pale orange or same color as the cap.

Stalk 2–8 cm long, 0.5–2.5 cm wide, somewhat smaller at base, smooth, light to dark orange, dry.

Odor mild to fruity.

Taste pleasant and mild.

Spore color light buff.

Habit and distribution: Solitary, scattered, numerous, sometimes growing in clumps, under hardwoods and mixed woods. Widely distributed. Fruiting in summer and fall.

Comments: Much work is being done to delineate species found in the United States. It is believed that many new species will soon be named. One of the reasons for this is that *Cantharellus* species grow symbiotically with specific trees and plants. This is a delicious edible and so are its closely related species.

Cantharellus subalbidus

edible and choice

A.H. Sm. & Morse
Western White Chanterelle

Cap 5–14 cm broad, convex, soon plane and slightly depressed, scaly in age, white.

Flesh firm, white.

Ridges blunt, extending a long way down the stalk, close, forked, with veins, white bruising yellow.

Stalk 2–5 cm long, 1–4 cm wide, equal, white, staining yellow or brown from handling or soil, dry.

Odor mild.

Taste pleasant.

Spore color white.

Habit and distribution: Single to several on the ground, under conifers and hardwoods. Found along the West Coast and in western North America. Fruiting in late summer and fall.

Comments: This is a robust, very good edible. Note the blunt ridges so typical of a chanterelle.

Craterellus fallax A.H. Sm.
Horn of Plenty

edible and choice

Fruiting body 4–15 cm tall.

Cap 2–8 cm broad, with a hollow, tubular depression, radially fibrillose, brown to blackish brown in age, dry.

Flesh very thin, brownish black.

Ridges smooth or nearly so, extending down the stalk almost to the base, smoky gray-brown.

Stalk very short, hollow, brown.

Odor pleasant.

Taste mild and pleasant.

Spore color light orange-buff.

Habit and distribution: Gregarious and often joined at the base, on ground in mixed conifer/ hardwoods or under hardwoods only. Widely distributed. Fruiting from early summer to fall.

Comments: *Craterellus cornucopioides* Pers. is very similar but has a white or faintly buff spore print. It is common in Europe but is also found in North America. Both species are choice edibles, but it takes a large number to make a meal. Fortunately, when you find one or two, you usually find a large number. They dry well.

Polyozellus multiplex Murrill   edible and good

Fruiting body in clusters 5–18 cm high, deep purple, violet-black, or blue-black.

Cap 2–10 cm broad, flat, smooth, with incurved margins, densely grouped together in large cespitose clusters.

Flesh soft, thick, blue-black.

Ridges low to almost smooth with many veins, similar to pores at times, extending down the stalk, pale violet.

Stalk 1–4 cm long, 1.0–2.4 cm wide, mostly grown together and fused, violet-black.

Odor not distinctive.

Taste mild and pleasant.

Spore color white.

Habit and distribution: In cespitose clusters under conifers (especially spruce and fir), often in blueberry patches. Found in northern North America. Fruiting in summer and fall.

Comments: I have found it in the Payette National Forest in central Idaho under pure Engelmann spruce and as far south as Colorado at high elevations under conifers. In Korea I have seen quantities for sale in the markets or along roadsides, collected under pine.

Gomphus clavatus (Fr.) Gray
Pig's Ear

edible with caution

Cap 3–15 cm broad, plane to depressed, margin lobed to deeply lobed, hairless to minutely scaly, buff to light purplish gray, dry.

Flesh firm, white or tinged cinnamon.

Ridges blunt, thick, interconnected by veins, frequently forked or almost like pores, extending down the stalk, light purple to light purplish brown to purple-gray.

Stalk 1–8 cm long, 1–2 cm wide, often arising from a compound base, blending at once into the funnel-shaped cap, purple-drab, base covered with white threads.

Odor none.

Taste mild.

Spore color yellowish orange.

Habit and distribution: Many growing from one cluster, under conifers. Widely distributed. Fruiting in late summer and fall.

Comments: This species is widely eaten; however, some people experience gastric upset, so be cautious.

Edible Agarics

All mushrooms included in this section have gills on the underside of the cap. Many agarics have a partial veil that covers the young gills. When the cap expands, the veil either separates at the cap margin, leaving a ring, or it pulls free from the stalk, leaving pieces hanging from the cap margin. In some genera in the group, the young button is surrounded by a universal veil. If the universal veil is composed of a tough membranous tissue, the expanding stalk splits it, leaving a discrete cup or volva surrounding the base. However, a soft, cottony universal veil simply clings to the bulb or base or leaves rings of tissue on the stalk and superficial scales and warts on the cap. These warts can be lifted off with a penknife, and it is evident that they are not part of the cap cuticle.

There are a number of families of agarics, and one of the important distinctions among them is the color of the spores. One should routinely make a spore print to be certain of a given species. Directions for making a spore print are covered in the How to Collect Mushrooms section (p. xii).

There are many excellent edibles among the world's agarics. However, there are some deadly poisonous species. Mistakes in identification could result in death. Before eating agaric mushrooms, always make a spore print to be sure of the type you have collected. And when in doubt, throw it out.

The agarics are the most difficult group of mushrooms to identify. I have, therefore, only listed a few really good ones that are quite easy to identify. I also list two deadly poisonous ones and one that is the most common mushroom ingested and reported to poison control centers in the United States. Again, do not eat more than one new fungus at a time. If you have a personal sensitivity to one or you mix up your collections, it will be difficult to determine which caused you to be sick. Always take some of the mushrooms that you ate with you when you seek medical attention so they can be identified.

Catathelasma imperialis (Fr.) Singer   edible and good
Potato Mushroom

Cap 15–40 cm broad, convex, broadly convex to plane in age, somewhat cracked at the center, margin incurved at first, cinnamon-buff, sometimes flushed olive to dark brown in age, viscid when wet, soon dry.

Flesh very thick, firm, white.

Gills extending down the stalk, broad, forked, buff to olive-gray.

Stalk 12–18 cm long, 6–8 cm wide, tapering to a dull point at the base, dull white.

Partial veil double, outer veil membranous and attached to upper cap margin, pinkish buff to brownish; inner veil softer, with clusters of hairs attached to lower margin of cap, leaving a persistent, superior, double ring on the stalk, which flares upward at first.

Odor not distinctive.

Taste mild.

Spore color white.

Habit and distribution: Single or several together under conifers, especially spruce and fir. Found in western North America, but most commonly in the western mountains. Fruiting in summer and fall.

Comments: The Alaskans call this the Potato Mushroom because the firmness of the flesh reminds them of a raw potato. They pickle it for use in winter. A sister species, *Catathelasma ventricosa* (Peck) Singer is similar, not nearly as large, pale gray to ash-gray, and also has a double partial veil. It grows from eastern Canada to Virginia but is rare. It is common in wet years in Idaho and the Pacific Northwest.

Clitocybe nuda (Fr.)
H.E. Bigelow & A.H. Sm.

edible and choice

Cap 4–15 cm broad, broadly convex, plane, with uplifted margin in age, sometimes with a low umbo, smooth, hairless, various shades of violet to violet-gray to cinnamon, with buff color in age, margin inrolled at first, dry.

Flesh usually firm, light lilac-buff.

Gills notched at the stalk, pale violet, pale lilac to sometimes brownish in age.

Stalk 3–6 (up to 10) cm long, 1.0–2.5 cm wide, equal, often with an oval basal bulb, pale violet, dull lavender covered below with scattered white hairs, dry.

Partial veil absent.

Odor pleasant, fairly fragrant.

Taste mild.

Spore color pinkish buff.

Habit and distribution: Single, but more often numerous, occasionally cespitose in needle duff or deep leaf litter under hardwoods and conifers, even in piles of leaves, in lawn grass, or around compost piles. Widely distributed. Fruiting in summer and fall.

Comments: This is a delicious edible species, often found in great quantity. It is also known as *Tricholoma nudum* and *Lepista nuda* in older guidebooks.

Coprinus comatus (Müll.:Fr.) Gray   edible and choice
Shaggy Mane, Inky Cap

Cap 5–15 cm broad, narrowly cylindric, expanding to bell-shaped, white, covered with flattened, reddish brown scales that recurve in age, dry.

Flesh soft, white.

Gills attached to the stalk, crowded, white when young, soon becoming black and inky as the gills gradually turn to ink in age.

Stalk 8–20 cm long, 1.0–2.5 cm wide, equal, white, smooth, dry.

Partial veil fibrous and soon free, leaving an often moveable ring.

Odor none.

Taste pleasant.

Spore color black.

Habit and distribution: Scattered or more often in groups on hard ground or grassy areas, growing from buried wood, often along roadsides. Widely distributed. Fruiting in cool, wet weather, most commonly in early spring and late fall.

Comments: Commonly called Shaggy Manes, these are among the most delightful of all edible mushrooms. The mushroom matures quickly and when the spores begin to mature, the gills turn black, starting from the margin of the cap and extending upward toward the stalk. The young buttons should be prepared for the table as quickly as possible after being collected. Mark the spot where you collected them, as they will occur in the same place for several years. Do not put collected mushrooms in the refrigerator; they will continue to turn inky. Cook them in a warm pan without any butter, since they will exude a great deal of liquid. This liquid can be frozen in ice cube trays and kept for months to be used in sauces. Once the Shaggy Manes have been heated, they may be kept for a few days in the refrigerator and used in any dish you want. They are especially good in soups, omelets, and sauces. The flavor is delicate, so don't overwhelm them with too many spices.

Flammulina velutipes (Fr.) Singer   edible and choice
Winter Mushroom, Velvet Foot, Enoki

Cap 1.5–10.0 cm broad, convex, nearly plane in age, margin often irregular, reddish yellow, reddish orange to reddish brown, viscid.

Flesh thick, white to yellowish.

Gills attached to the stalk, subdistant, broad, cream to yellowish, edges minutely hairy.

Stalk 2–8 cm long, 0.3–1.2 cm wide, slightly narrower at base, yellowish at top, rest with dense, velvety, short brown to blackish brown hairs, tough, hollow in age.

Partial veil absent.

Odor pleasant.

Taste mild.

Spore color white.

Habit and distribution: Single but most often in cespitose clusters on dead wood or living trees. Widely distributed. Fruiting in cold weather in winter, spring, and late fall.

Comments: Often fruiting in late winter after warm spells. We have found this every month of the year from Alaska to New Hampshire, but it always favors cool periods of weather. It is widely cultivated as food, especially in Asia, under the name *enokitake*. The mushrooms are grown in the dark and so have no color. Note the picture below, on the right. This specimen from the wild has very tough stalks, which should be discarded before cooking.

Lactarius deliciosus (Fr.) Gray
Orange Milk Lactarius

edible and choice

Cap 5–15 cm broad, convex to broadly convex, margin incurved, orange or carrot-colored mixed with dingy green, usually more green with age, sometimes zoned, viscid to sticky in wet weather.
Flesh very light orange, staining green in age.
Latex carrot-colored, leaving green stains, especially when cut.
Gills extending slightly down the stalk, close, bright orange, staining green in age or after injury.
Stalk 2–6 cm long, 1.5–3.0 cm wide, equal, narrow just at base, smooth, dry, light orange, turning green when handled or in age.
Odor not distinctive.
Taste mild, in time slightly acrid.
Spore color buff.
Habit and distribution: Single to scattered under conifer or mixed hardwood conifer forests. Widely distributed. Fruiting in late summer and fall.
Comments: This is a delicious edible that is easily identified by its green staining and orange latex. The best way to cook these is in butter. Other edible species in this group, which also have brightly colored latex, are *L. rubrilacteus, L. indigo,* and *L. salmoneus.* Another species worth trying is *L. volemus.* Look for descriptions in *North American Mushrooms.*

Marasmius oreades Fr.   edible and choice

Cap 2–6 cm broad, convex, bell-shaped in age, smooth, hairless, margin somewhat longitudinally striped in age, light tan to light brown or reddish brown, fading in age, dry.

Flesh thin, watery, white.

Gills attached to the stalk, nearly free, fairly well separated, veined, broad, light buff.

Stalk 3–7 cm long, 0.3–0.5 cm wide, equal, tough, buff at top to reddish brown at base, minute hairs especially dense over the base, dry.

Partial veil absent.

Odor fragrant.

Taste mild and pleasant.

Spore color white to buff.

Habit and distribution: Grows in partial or complete fairy rings on lawns, pastures, golf courses, and grasslands of various kinds. Widely distributed. Fruiting in spring, summer, and fall.

Comments: Fairy rings increase in size each year as the mycelium grows out to decompose the dead parts of the new grass. This mushroom is a very good edible with a flavor that enhances vegetables, gravies, or stir-fry. Use caution eating mushrooms collected along highways because they often contain lead, cadmium, or other exhaust compounds. I have seen multiple fairy rings there following heavy summer thunderstorms.

Pleurotus ostreatus Fr.
Oyster Mushroom

edible and good

Cap 2–30 cm broad, 0.8–8.0 cm wide, oyster shell, fan-shaped to broadly convex, sometimes lobed or wavy, smooth, hairless, white, pale pink to light yellow-brown, moist.

Flesh firm, thick, dull white.

Gills extending to the blunt point of attachment, fairly well separated, broad, thick, veined, white.

Stalk usually absent, if present 0.5–1.5 cm long, 0.5–1.0 cm thick, off-center, often dense, white pubescent with white hairs around base, dry.

Odor of anise or fragrant and fruity.

Taste mild and pleasant.

Spore color white, buff to pale pink.

Habit and distribution: Rarely single, usually in large, overlapping clusters on branches, logs, and stumps of hardwoods and conifers. Widely distributed, but most commonly in eastern North America. Fruiting during or following wet weather in spring and fall, often in late fall.

Comments: This fungus is found almost any time conditions are right. Two closely related species are known. *Pleurotus pulmonarius* (Fr.) Quél. is the most common species in western North America, found on conifers, and cannot be distinguished from *P. ostreatus* in the field. *Pleurotus populinus* Hilber & O. K. Mill., found on cottonwood and aspen in northern North America, also cannot be distinguished. All three are good edibles.

Russula xerampelina Fr.
Woodland Russula

edible and good

Cap 3–16 cm broad, broadly convex to convex-depressed, margin longitudinally striped, purplish red, carmine red, maroon, or lighter, even olive at the margin, viscid at first, soon dry and felt-like to touch.

Flesh firm, white.

Gills attached to the stalk, close, thick, no short gills intermixed with others, cream, yellow to orange-yellow, turning gray when dried.

Stalk 3–8 cm long, 1.5–3.3 (up to 5.0) cm wide, club-shaped or even bulbous at the base, white, flushed pinkish, wrinkled, grooved, or even faintly netlike, hollow in age.

Odor of crab or lobster, usually quite strong but stronger when dried.

Taste mild.

Spore color yellow.

Habit and distribution: Scattered or in groups in conifer forests. Widely distributed. Fruiting in summer and fall.

Comments: Nonedible species in the genus also have the crab or lobster odor, so it is important to go collecting with those who know their species. *Russula xerampelina* is one of the best edibles in this genus.

Stropharia rugosoannulata
Farl.: Murrill
edible and choice

King Stropharia

Cap 5.5–25.0 cm broad, robust, convex to plane in age, dark red, red-brown to purple-red, light brownish red in age, viscid.

Flesh firm, white.

Gills attached to the stalk, close, broad white to gray but soon purple in age.

Stalk 7–14 cm long, 1.4–3.5 cm wide, equal to club-shaped, white above the partial veil, below smooth, white, dry.

Partial veil a superior, white, flaring membranous ring, which soon becomes starlike, with conspicuous white cogs on the under surface.

Odor pleasant, faintly of meal or grain.

Taste mild.

Spore color dark violet-brown.

Habit and distribution: Several to many in mulch, garden beds, and other cultivated areas. Widely distributed. Fruiting from spring to fall.

Comments: This choice edible is found throughout North America in mulch beds and areas under some sort of cultivation. It is not found in natural habitats in North America. It can be very robust and is grown commercially in Europe. It is easy to identify because of the characteristic partial veil and red cap.

Tricholoma magnivelare

edible and choice

(Peck) Redhead
American Matsutake

Cap 8–20 cm broad, broadly convex, plane in age, white with flattened, brown scales, developing over the center, streaked with brown hairs elsewhere, margin a narrow, white inrolled flap, tacky to moist.

Flesh firm, white.

Gills attached to the stalk, crowded, broad, white, bruising pinkish to reddish brown.

Stalk 6–18 cm long, 2–4 cm wide, tapering somewhat toward base, smooth and white above the ring, below covered with reddish brown scales and hairs in age, sticky when wet, soon dry.

Partial veil membranous, white, leaving a persistent, skirt-like ring, soon stained reddish brown on the edge and outside.

Odor spicy, sweet even in button stage.

Taste pleasant.

Spore color white.

Habit and distribution: Scattered to abundant under mixed conifers. Widely distributed, but abundant and common along the Pacific Coast and locally elsewhere. Fruiting in the fall, except along the West Coast, where it fruits from October to early February. It has been recorded in Maine and also Texas.

Comments: This fungus is highly prized as a choice edible along the West Coast. Commercial pickers are seen commonly in the national forests; they export their finds to Japan and elsewhere.

Poisonous Agarics

Amanita virosa (Fr.) Quél.   **deadly poisonous**
Death Angel, Destroying Angel

Cap: 3.0–9.5 cm broad, conic to ovoid, convex to plane, pure white, smooth, viscid when wet to sticky, margin smooth, not ribbed or only obscurely so, no volval warts.
Flesh firm, white.
Gills free, close to narrowly spaced in age, narrow, white.
Stalk 14–24 cm long, 1.0–2.3 cm wide, enlarging gradually to a club-shaped base, white, dry, finely fibrous above ring, hairy below.
Volva white, membranous, persistent, sac-like, and free from the stalk, often 3–4 cm high.
Partial veil membranous, white, smooth, faintly striate on upper surface, leaving a tattered or skirt-like superior ring, which upon occasion is almost missing.
Odor none or slightly unpleasant.
Do not taste this fungus.
Spore color white.
Habit and distribution: Solitary but usually several together under oaks and hardwood forests or in mixed woods. Widely distributed in eastern North America. Fruiting in summer and fall.
Comments: There are at least four well-known species of white Amanitas. All should be considered deadly poisonous. *Amanita ocreata* Peck is found under live oak in California, Oregon, and Washington and fruits from January to March. *Amanita bisporigera* G.F. Atk. is found in the eastern and

northern United States and Canada and usually fruits in spring or early summer. *Amanita volvata* (Peck) Martin is another white species with a thick, sac-like volva, and it is found in the southeastern United States. Note the button stage in the photo. It can be confused with a small puffball; this is why it is important to cut all puffball look-alikes from the top to the point of attachment to the ground. If the form of a mushroom appears, you might have an *Amanita* and not a puffball. (If the interior appears like cream cheese and has no mushroom-like appearance, it is a puffball.)

The toxins in the deadly poisonous Amanitas are cyclopeptides, which kill liver cells, often causing the victim to require a liver transplant. The symptoms are a pleasant-tasting mushroom, no problems for four to eight hours, great pain, then recovery for another few hours, only to have the pain return. This comes from the re-cycling of the toxins from kidneys to liver, through the system, only to return and kill more liver cells. This cycle continues until death occurs. Remember the rules for eating mushrooms discussed in the introduction of this book (p. xiv) and always take the remaining mushrooms to the emergency room for identification when seeking treatment.

Amanita phalloides Fr.   **deadly poisonous**
Green Death Cap

Cap 7–15 cm broad, convex, viscid, smooth, pale yellow-green, brownish green to green, with flattened radiating hairs, margin smooth, universal patches on surface.

Flesh firm, white to light green just below the cap cuticle.

Gills free, close, broad, white.

Stalk 8–14 cm long, 1–2 cm wide, enlarging somewhat toward the base, white, smooth.

Volva membranous, persistent, sac-like, white.

Partial veil membranous, remains a superior ring hanging skirt-like on the stalk.

Odor slightly disagreeable.

Do not taste this fungus.

Spore color white.

Habit and distribution: Several to numerous, on ground, under or near European trees, such as Norway spruce, or in tree plantations established in America. Known from New Jersey, Virginia, Maryland, Minnesota, Oregon, Washington, and California, but likely to be found around all shipping ports. Fruiting in summer and early fall.

Comments: This species was introduced to the United States in the early part of the last century on European tree root stock, and it is now widespread, even mycorrhizal with local trees. It is as deadly as the white Amanitas. The young buttons can be easily mistaken for the Paddy Straw Mushroom, *Volvariella volvacea* (Bull.:Fr.) Singer. Asian immigrants living on the West Coast have been poisoned by *Amanita phalloides* when they have mistaken it for the edible *Volvariella* from their homelands. Volvariellas have a pink spore color, not white. I do not recommend eating any Amanitas even though some are reported to be edible. Better to be safe than sorry.

Chlorophyllum molybdites Massee   **very poisonous**
Green-Spored Lepiota

Cap 7–30 cm broad, conic, convex with a center knob to nearly plane in age, white with numerous slightly raised scales tinted buff to cinnamon, dry.

Flesh firm, white, dingy reddish where bruised.

Gills free, close, broad, white, becoming green in age, bruising yellow to brownish.

Stalk 10–25 cm long, 1.0–2.5 cm wide, enlarging toward the base, smooth, white with brownish stains over base.

Partial veil a thick, white, superior ring with fringed edge, discoloring brownish beneath.

Odor none.

Do not taste this species.

Spore color green.

Habit and distribution: Scattered or in partial or complete fairy rings in lawns and grasslands, during or after wet rainy periods. Widely distributed throughout North America, including Hawaii. Fruiting in spring, but mostly late summer and fall.

Comments: This fungus is one of most common causes of mushroom poisoning reported to poison control centers. Many species of *Lepiota,* of which this is one, are edible, so care must be taken to make a clear identification of the scaly-capped species. Most of the rest do not grow in fairy rings and do not give a green spore print. The gills of the Green-Spored Lepiota are white until the spores mature, so make sure to use the most mature specimens when getting a spore print. The gills turn green from the green spores.

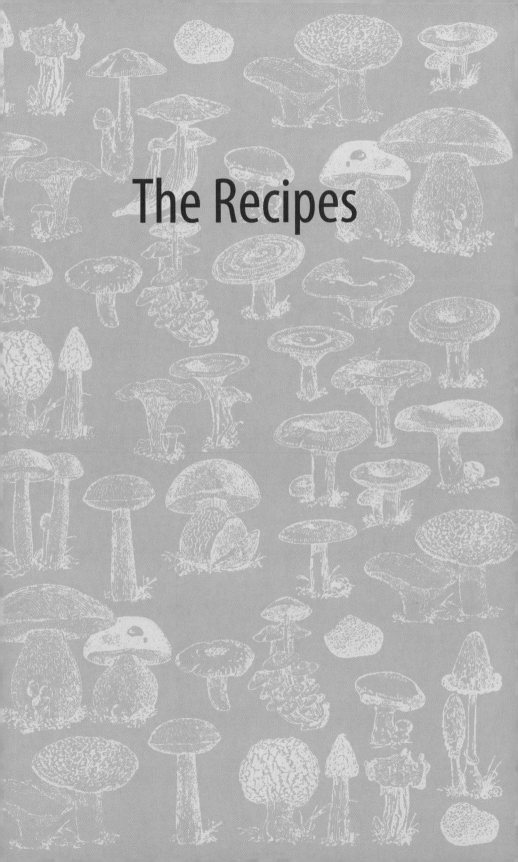

The Recipes

Appetizers

Hot Mushroom Dip Especial

1 pound mushrooms, very finely chopped
1 stick (8 tablespoons) butter or margarine, softened
1 tablespoon lemon juice
2 tablespoons minced onion
1 pound sour cream
2 tablespoons chicken bouillon granules (or 2 cubes dissolved)
Salt and pepper to taste
2 tablespoons flour
Chips, crackers, or fresh vegetables

1. Sauté mushrooms in a large frying pan on medium-high heat with 6 tablespoons of butter and the lemon juice until soft.

2. Simmer for 5 to 10 minutes.

3. Add onion, sour cream, bouillon granules, and salt and pepper and simmer for 5 to 10 minutes more.

4. Mix remaining butter and enough flour to make a paste to be used to thicken the dip.

5. Add the paste to the hot mixture and stir until thickened.

6. Serve in a fondue pot or chafing dish with chips, crackers, or fresh vegetables.

YIELDS 4–5 CUPS

This recipe may be used as a filling for crepes or omelets, as a sauce for baked chicken, as a vegetable dip, or any other way you might want.

Bacon Mushroom Bites

4 slices bacon
1 small onion, chopped
¼ cup chopped black olives
½ cup grated Parmesan cheese
1 tablespoon Worcestershire sauce
32 small mushrooms
2 tablespoons dry bread crumbs

1. Preheat the oven for broiling.

2. Fry bacon until crispy, then crumble it.

3. Sauté the onion in bacon grease over medium-high heat until translucent; add olives, cheese, and Worcestershire sauce.

4. Combine bacon and sautéed ingredients. Stuff mushrooms with this mixture and sprinkle with crumbs.

5. Broil stuffed mushrooms until hot and bubbly.

SERVES 12

Mushroom Caviar

1 cup chopped scallions
2 tablespoons butter or margarine
2 cups chopped mushrooms
1 tablespoon lemon juice
Pinch of cayenne pepper
½ teaspoon soy sauce
2 tablespoons chopped fresh dill or parsley
⅔ cup yogurt
Salt and pepper to taste
Chopped pecans
Paprika

1. Sauté scallions in butter over medium-high heat for 1 minute.

2. Add mushrooms, lemon juice, cayenne, and soy sauce, and sauté for 4 minutes.

3. Remove from heat and stir in dill or parsley and yogurt. Season with salt and pepper.

4. Chill for at least 2 hours.

5. Transfer to a serving bowl and garnish with pecans and paprika. Serve with crackers.

YIELDS 3–4 CUPS

Puffballs Parmesan

1 large fresh puffball
Flour (enough to coat puffball slices)
1 egg, beaten
1 tablespoon water
Parmesan cheese, finely grated
Butter or margarine

1. Slice puffball into ½-inch slabs.

2. Coat puffball slices with flour. Shake lightly to remove any excess.

3. Mix the egg and water. Dip the floured puffball slices into this mixture.

4. Dip puffball slices in grated cheese.

5. Heat butter in large frying pan over medium-high heat and fry puffballs until golden brown.

6. Cut puffball slices into small pieces and place on a plate with toothpicks.

SERVES 8–12 AS FINGER FOOD, DEPENDING ON THE SIZE OF THE PUFFBALL

When young and edible, a puffball should be pure white inside. It should look as though you have cut through a block of cream cheese. It should be fresh, not one that has been in the refrigerator for 3 or 4 days. It may look fresh but it will have spoiled without changing color.

Ruth's Marinated Mushrooms

> 1¼ cups olive oil or vegetable oil
> ¾ cup soy sauce
> ¾ cup malt vinegar
> 2 garlic cloves, minced
> ¼ teaspoon black pepper
> 1 pound mushrooms, quartered

1. Whisk together olive oil, soy sauce, malt vinegar, garlic, and pepper.

2. Add mushrooms and stir to coat.

3. Refrigerate for at least 7 hours, stirring every few hours.

4. Serve with toothpicks.

SERVES 10–12

Note: These may be kept in the refrigerator for up to 3 weeks.

Ruth's Marinated Mushrooms make a nice addition to any main dish, as well as being a great appetizer.

Stuffed Mushrooms á la Hutton

1 pound medium-size mushrooms
Lemon juice
1 (10-ounce) package frozen chopped spinach, thawed and juice
  squeezed out
1 cup cottage cheese
1 clove garlic, minced
1 teaspoon pepper
⅔ cup grated Parmesan cheese

1. Preheat oven to 400°F.

2. Remove stems from mushrooms (save for other uses). Brush caps with lemon juice.

3. Combine thawed but not cooked spinach, cottage cheese, garlic, pepper, and ⅓ cup Parmesan cheese. Mix thoroughly.

4. Spoon spinach mixture into caps; top with remaining Parmesan cheese.

5. Bake for 10 minutes and serve hot.

SERVES 12

Beef-Stuffed Mushrooms

    1 pound medium-size mushrooms, stems removed
    2 tablespoons butter or margarine
    1 pound ground round
    1 garlic clove, minced
    4 tablespoons chopped fresh parsley
    1 (8-ounce) can tomato sauce
    ½ cup bread crumbs
    2 eggs, slightly beaten
    4 tablespoons grated Parmesan cheese

1. Preheat oven to 350°F.

2. Sauté mushrooms in butter over medium-high heat until slightly cooked. Set aside. Reserve any liquid.

3. Sauté beef, garlic, and parsley over medium-high heat. Remove from heat.

4. Add tomato sauce, bread crumbs, beaten eggs, and Parmesan cheese to the meat mixture. Stir to combine thoroughly.

5. Stuff mushrooms with meat mixture.

6. Pour sauté liquid into a baking dish.

7. Place mushrooms right side up in the baking dish and bake for 20 minutes.

SERVES 10–12

Mushroom Snacks

>   *2 shallots, finely chopped*
>   *2 cups very finely chopped mushrooms*
>   *Small amount of butter or margarine*
>   *¾ pound softened cream cheese*
>   *½ teaspoon Worcestershire sauce*
>   *¼ teaspoon garlic powder*
>   *1 loaf cocktail bread, sliced*

1. Sauté shallots and mushrooms in a very small amount of butter. Remove from heat.

2. Add cream cheese, Worcestershire sauce, and garlic powder to mushroom mixture.

3. Mix well, and let mixture chill in the refrigerator overnight.

4. Spread mushroom mixture on bread slices and broil until bubbly. Serve warm.

SERVES 10–12

Cheesy Mushroom Squares or Sticks

1 stick (8 tablespoons) butter or margarine
½ pound sliced mushrooms
1 medium onion, chopped
2 garlic cloves, chopped
1 green pepper, chopped
10 eggs, beaten
2 cups cottage cheese
1 pound Monterey Jack cheese, shredded
½ cup flour
1 teaspoon baking powder
¾ teaspoon nutmeg
¾ teaspoon dry basil
¾ teaspoon salt

1. Preheat oven to 350°F.

2. Melt butter in a frying pan and sauté mushrooms, onion, garlic, and pepper over medium-high heat until onions are translucent. Remove from heat.

3. In a large bowl, mix together beaten eggs, cottage cheese, Monterey Jack cheese, flour, baking powder, nutmeg, basil, and salt.

4. Combine the egg mixture with the mushroom mixture.

5. Pour the mixture into an ungreased 17½ x 11½-inch jelly-roll pan. Bake for 35 minutes or until set and golden brown on top.

6. Let cool 15–20 minutes before cutting. For a luncheon, cut into squares and serve with a salad and rolls. For sticks, cut into pieces approximately ¾ inch wide and 3 inches long. The squares or sticks will keep in the refrigerator for 2 days and can be reheated in the microwave.

YIELDS 8 DOZEN STICKS

Teriyaki Mushrooms

2 tablespoons sugar
2 tablespoons soy sauce
1 tablespoon white wine vinegar
1 tablespoon olive oil or vegetable oil
¼–½ teaspoon red pepper flakes
¼–½ teaspoon ground ginger
¼ teaspoon garlic powder
24 small mushrooms, quartered
2 teaspoons sliced scallions

Combine sugar, soy sauce, vinegar, oil, red pepper flakes, ginger, and garlic powder in a medium saucepan. Mix well. Add mushrooms and scallions and cook over medium heat, stirring until heated through.

SERVES 4–6

These mushrooms would pair very nicely with a Chinese entree. They may be served hot or cold and, like many recipes made with mushrooms, they are very nutritious.

Maxine's Herbed Mushrooms

> *3 tablespoons olive or vegetable oil*
> *¾ pound sliced or quartered big mushrooms*
> *½ teaspoon salt*
> *¼ teaspoon dry marjoram*
> *½ teaspoon dry sweet basil*
> *¼ teaspoon garlic powder*
> *½ cup burgundy wine*
> *1 lemon wedge*

1. Heat oil until smoking hot and add mushrooms. Sauté until partially cooked.

2. Add salt, marjoram, sweet basil, garlic powder, and burgundy wine. Squeeze lemon into pan and then throw in peel.

3. Simmer until liquid is reduced by one half. Let cool and serve with toothpicks.

SERVES 10–12

Broccoli Dip

½ cup finely chopped mushrooms
1 garlic clove, minced
1 stick (8 tablespoons) butter or margarine
2 (5-ounce) jars Cheez Whiz
1 (1-ounce) package Lipton dry onion soup mix
1 (10.5-ounce) can undiluted mushroom soup
2 (10-ounce) packages frozen chopped broccoli
1 tablespoon dry minced onion

1. Sauté mushrooms and garlic in butter over medium-high heat until mushrooms are soft.

2. Combine Cheez Whiz, soup mix, and soup in a saucepan and heat.

3. Cook broccoli in unsalted water according to directions on package; drain.

4. Combine mushroom mixture, Cheez Whiz mixture, broccoli, and onion. Serve warm with chips or tortilla chips.

SERVES 10–12

Sausage-Stuffed Mushrooms

16 large mushrooms
3 tablespoons olive oil
6 ounces sweet sausage, crumbled
1 garlic clove, minced
¼ cup water
¼ cup Parmesan cheese
2 teaspoons minced fresh parsley

1. Preheat oven to 350°F.

2. Remove stems from mushrooms, then chop stems finely. Reserve caps.

3. Heat oil in a medium frying pan. Sauté mushroom stems, sausage, and garlic in hot oil over medium-high heat until lightly browned.

4. Add water, Parmesan, and parsley to mushroom-sausage mixture, and mix well. Remove from heat.

5. Use the mushroom-sausage mixture to stuff the mushroom caps. Place caps in a shallow pan and bake for 20 minutes.

SERVES 6–8

Mushroom and Cream Cheese Spread

1 ounce dried mushrooms
1 large onion, quartered
¾ pound fresh button mushrooms
2 tablespoons olive oil or vegetable oil
½ teaspoon tarragon
½ teaspoon salt
¼ teaspoon pepper
1 tablespoon brandy
1 tablespoon lemon juice
1 (3-ounce) package cream cheese
Fresh chives or parsley (optional)

1. Soak dried mushrooms in a small bowl filled with enough boiling water to cover for 15 minutes or until mushrooms are softened. Drain and rinse well to remove any sand. Squeeze mushrooms dry and trim off stems.

2. Place reconstituted mushrooms and onion in food processor. Pulse until finely chopped, then set aside.

3. Put fresh mushrooms in food processor and pulse until finely chopped.

4. Heat oil in medium-size frying pan over medium-high heat. Cook mushroom-onion mixture for 3 minutes.

5. Add fresh mushrooms, tarragon, salt, and pepper. Cook 8 to 10 minutes or until all liquid is evaporated. Stir in brandy and cook 1 minute more.

6. Remove frying pan from heat. Add lemon juice and cream cheese, stirring until smooth.

7. Transfer spread to a bowl, cover, and refrigerate overnight for best flavor.

8. Garnish spread with chives or parsley if desired. Serve with Melba toasts, wheat crackers, pita chips, or assorted vegetables. Spread can be held in refrigerator for up to 5 days. Recipe can be doubled, tripled, or quadrupled.

YIELDS 2 CUPS

This spread is also wonderful smeared on ham slices. Roll the slices, then cut them into small pieces and serve as an appetizer. If you are having baked potatoes, try putting a tablespoon of the spread on them while they are still hot.

Spinach, Artichokes, and Mushrooms in Puff Pastry

1 (17-ounce) package frozen puff pastry
1 (10-ounce) package frozen chopped spinach, thawed
¼ pound mushrooms, finely chopped
4 tablespoons butter or margarine
1 (14-ounce) can artichoke hearts, drained and chopped
½ cup mayonnaise
½ cup grated Parmesan cheese
1 teaspoon each onion powder and garlic powder
¼ teaspoon pepper

1. Thaw pastry at room temperature for 30 minutes. Drain spinach well, pressing between layers of paper towels.

2. Cook mushrooms in butter over medium-high heat until they are well done and most of the liquid has been absorbed.

3. In a large bowl, combine spinach, mushrooms, artichoke hearts, mayonnaise, Parmesan, onion and garlic powders, and pepper.

4. Unfold thawed pastry and place on a lightly floured surface or heavy-duty plastic wrap.

5. Spread one-fourth of the spinach mixture evenly over one pastry sheet, leaving a half-inch border on all sides.

6. Roll up the pastry, jelly-roll fashion, pressing the seam to seal. Wrap the roll in heavy-duty plastic wrap.

7. Continue spreading the spinach mixture on pastry sheets, rolling up, and wrapping in plastic until all ingredients are used up.

8. Put wrapped pastry rolls in the freezer for 30 minutes. (Rolls can be kept in freezer for up to 3 months.) Preheat oven to 400°F. Cut the frozen pastry rolls into ½-inch-thick slices. Bake for 20 minutes, longer if still frozen.

Yields 4 dozen

Easy Mushroom Squares

3 cups finely chopped mushrooms (approximately 8 ounces)
¼ cup finely chopped onion
½ teaspoon Worcestershire sauce
10 tablespoons butter or margarine
2 cups Bisquick baking mix
¼ cup boiling water
1 (3-ounce) package cream cheese, softened
¼ cup grated Parmesan cheese

1. Preheat oven to 350°F. Grease a 13 x 9-inch pan.

2. Sauté mushrooms, onion, and Worcestershire sauce in 2 tablespoons butter over medium-high heat until brown.

3. Mix baking mix and remaining 8 tablespoons butter in a small bowl until it forms small pieces about the size of peas. Add water and beat until soft dough forms.

4. Spread dough in prepared pan and spread cream cheese over dough. Top with mushroom mixture and Parmesan cheese.

5. Bake until crust is golden brown in color, approximately 20–30 minutes.

6. Cut into 1½-inch squares and serve immediately. Refrigerate any leftover squares and reheat in the microwave before serving.

YIELDS APPROXIMATELY **54** SQUARES

Crab-Filled Mushrooms

1 pound mushrooms
4 tablespoons butter or margarine
1 tablespoon minced onion
2 slices white bread
2 eggs, beaten
2 tablespoons sour cream
1 (6.5-ounce) can king crabmeat
2 tablespoons chopped fresh parsley
Salt and pepper to taste
Paprika

1. Preheat oven to 350°F.

2. Remove stems from mushrooms and chop finely to make 1 cup.

3. Melt butter in a frying pan. Sauté mushroom caps in butter over medium-high heat. Place in a buttered baking dish.

4. Remove crusts from bread and tear into crumbs. Combine with mushroom stems and add onion.

5. Add eggs, sour cream, crabmeat, parsley, and salt and pepper to mushroom-bread mixture. Mix well.

6. Spoon mixture into mushroom caps. Sprinkle with paprika and bake for 10–12 minutes. Serve immediately.

SERVES 10–12

Mushroom-Filled Cream Cheese Turnovers

3 (3-ounce) packages cream cheese
10 tablespoons butter or margarine
1½ cups plus 1½ tablespoons flour, sifted
½ onion, finely chopped
¼ pound mushrooms, finely chopped
⅛ teaspoon thyme
¼ teaspoon salt
⅛ teaspoon pepper
½ cup sour cream

1. Mix cream cheese and 8 tablespoons butter together. Add 1½ cups flour and work it with your hands or with a pastry blender.

2. Form pastry into a flattened ball and wrap in waxed paper. Chill for at least an hour.

3. Preheat oven to 450°F.

4. Melt remaining 2 tablespoons butter and sauté chopped onion over medium-high heat, until lightly browned.

5. Add mushrooms, thyme, salt, and pepper, and cook for about 5 minutes, stirring frequently. Sprinkle with remaining 1½ tablespoons flour and stir.

6. Reduce heat and stir in sour cream. Continue to cook, stirring constantly, until thickened.

7. Allow mushroom mixture to cool, then chill for 20 minutes. Roll out pastry to about ⅛ inch thick and cut out 3-inch rounds.

8. Place about ½ teaspoon filling on each round. Wet edges and fold over, pressing the edges with a fork. Prick the top crusts with the fork. Chill for 20 minutes.

9. Bake turnovers for about 15 minutes.

SERVES 10–12

Soups

Cold Cucumber and Mushroom Soup

3 large cucumbers
1 pound mushrooms, chopped
3 shallots, chopped
3 tablespoons butter or margarine
3 tablespoons flour
2½ cups chicken broth
1 teaspoon dill weed, plus more for garnish
2 teaspoons lemon juice
2 cups half and half
Salt and pepper to taste

1. Peel and halve cucumbers. Remove seeds and chop.

2. Sauté cucumbers, mushrooms, and shallots in butter over medium-high heat until soft.

3. Stir in flour, then chicken broth, dill weed, and lemon juice. Cook until thickened.

4. Transfer soup to blender and puree.

5. Add half and half to pureed soup. Add salt and pepper to taste. Chill for up to 8 hours.

6. Serve soup very cold. Top with a light sprinkling of dill weed.

SERVES 8

Cumin, Zucchini, and Mushroom Soup

4 tablespoons butter or margarine
½ cup chopped mushrooms
1 small onion, minced
2 garlic cloves, minced
1½ pounds zucchini, chopped
¼ cup white wine
2 cups chicken stock (or vegetable or beef stock)
2 tablespoons grated Parmesan cheese
1 teaspoon cumin (or more to taste)
Dash of pepper

1. Melt butter in a large saucepan and sauté mushrooms, onion, and garlic over medium-high heat for 2 to 4 minutes, stirring constantly.

2. Add zucchini, wine, and stock. Simmer 10 minutes.

3. Transfer soup to blender and puree.

4. Return soup to pan and add Parmesan cheese, cumin, and pepper. Heat for 3 to 4 minutes. Serve soup hot or chilled.

SERVES 4–6

Some ingredients, such as lemon juice, dill, and tarragon, particularly enhance mushrooms' flavor. Shallots (used instead of garlic) add a special flavor to your dishes and don't overpower them. Some cooks add a lot of garlic or soy sauce, which overpowers the mushroom flavors. You want to taste the delicate flavors of the mushrooms, not the spices you use, so limit the amount of seasoning.

Hungarian Mushroom Soup

> 1 tablespoon butter or margarine
> 1 small onion, chopped
> ½ pound mushrooms, cut into pieces
> Fresh parsley, chopped
> Hungarian paprika to taste
> 2 tablespoons flour
> 3–4 cups water
> 2 carrots, peeled and cut into pieces
> 1 parsnip, peeled and cut into pieces
> Salt to taste
> ¼ cup rice
> ½ cup sour cream, plus more for garnish (optional)

1. Melt butter in a large pan.

2. Sauté onion over medium-high heat until translucent, then add mushrooms. Cover and steam for 1 to 2 minutes.

3. Add chopped parsley to pan. Sprinkle with paprika and flour and cook for 1 minute more.

4. Add water, carrots, parsnip, and salt.

5. Bring to a boil. Add rice and boil for about 15 minutes longer or until rice is tender.

6. Stir in sour cream and serve immediately.

7. You can add a dollop of sour cream on top and sprinkle with a little more paprika.

SERVES 4

Lemon Dilly Morel Soup

1 stick (8 tablespoons) butter or margarine
1 pound dried morels, reconstituted in hot water
½ cup minced shallots
Salt and pepper to taste
4 cups chicken stock
2 cups lemon juice
Fresh dill, minced, to taste

1. Melt butter in the bottom of a Dutch oven.

2. Add reconstituted morels, reserving liquid used to reconstitute.

3. Add minced shallots and salt and pepper.

4. Cook until shallots are translucent.

5. Strain mushroom liquid and add some to the soup.

6. Add chicken stock, lemon juice, and dill and simmer over low heat until hot.

7. Serve soup with some extra dill for garnish.

SERVES 6–8

Note: This recipe uses a lot of lemon, but it adds great flavor to the dish.

Swiss Cheese, Mushroom, and Potato Soup

1 cup dried morels or porcini
1 cup boiling water, lightly salted
3 medium potatoes, chopped
1 small onion, finely chopped
3 tablespoons butter, melted
3 tablespoons flour
3 tablespoons chopped fresh parsley
Salt and pepper to taste
6 cups milk
1 cup grated Swiss cheese
Chives or croutons

1. Reconstitute mushrooms in boiling water until soft. (Mushrooms can be crumbled before placing in the water, which will make them easier to work with.)

2. In a stockpot, and using the same liquid in which the mushrooms were reconstituted, boil the potatoes, onion, and mushrooms for 20 minutes. Mash without draining and set aside.

3. To make the white sauce, mix the butter, flour, parsley, and salt and pepper in a large saucepan. Add the milk and cook, stirring, until the mixture thickens and bubbles.

4. Add the white sauce to the potato mixture. Add the Swiss cheese and cook until cheese is partially melted.

5. Sprinkle the soup with chives or croutons. Serve immediately.

SERVES 8–10

Mushroom Asparagus Soup

1 tablespoon butter or margarine
3 green onions, thinly sliced, including tops
¼ pound mushrooms, sliced
1¾ cups chicken broth
1½–2 pounds asparagus
1 cup milk
¼ cup salsa
Salt and pepper to taste
½ cup shredded Monterey Jack cheese

1. Melt butter in 4-quart saucepan over medium heat. Add onions and mushrooms, and sauté over medium-high heat for approximately 3 minutes.

2. Add broth and whole asparagus spears. Bring to a boil and simmer until asparagus is tender but not limp. Snip off the tips of 8 spears and reserve. Continue to simmer until asparagus is very tender, about 5 minutes more.

3. Transfer broth and asparagus to a blender. Add milk and salsa and puree.

4. Return soup to pan and cook over medium heat until steaming hot. Add salt and pepper to taste.

5. Ladle soup into 4 bowls and sprinkle with cheese. Garnish with reserved asparagus tips.

SERVES 4

Salsa adds spice to this soup. Though I've suggested ¼ cup as a starting point, you can use as much or as little as you would like. Some people like it hot and some people do not.

Asian Pork and Mushroom Soup

2 (13-ounce) cans chicken broth
⅓ pound lean pork, finely diced
1 garlic clove, mashed
1 tablespoon soy sauce
¼ cup sliced mushrooms
¼ cup sliced water chestnuts
¼ cup frozen green peas

1. In a large saucepan, combine chicken broth, pork, garlic, and soy sauce. Simmer for 10 minutes.

2. Add mushrooms, water chestnuts, and peas, and simmer 2 more minutes.

3. Serve soup with fried rice.

SERVES 4–6

> This soup is a good accompaniment to a Chinese buffet-style meal. Or, for a nice lunch, serve this soup and pot stickers or spring rolls.

Polish Mushroom Soup

¼ pound dried porcini mushrooms
3½ cups hot water
3 quarts beef or chicken broth
1 cup pearl barley, rinsed
1½ cups sour cream, plus more for garnish
2 tablespoons flour
Salt and pepper to taste
½ cup minced fresh parsley

1. Reconstitute mushrooms in water for 1 hour. Drain the mushrooms, reserving liquid, and chop mushrooms into ½-inch pieces.

2. Combine broth and mushrooms in a 5- or 6-quart pan. Add the liquid from reconstituting the mushrooms.

3. Add barley. Cover and bring soup to a boil. Reduce heat and simmer for approximately 1 hour.

4. Mix 1½ cups sour cream with flour, and add slowly to soup, stirring constantly. Bring to a boil. Add salt and pepper to taste.

5. Serve soup with a spoonful of sour cream and sprinkle parsley on top. The soup can be made ahead and reheated before serving.

SERVES 8–10

Mushroom and Butternut Squash Soup

2 teaspoons olive oil or vegetable oil
1 leek, white part only, thinly sliced
2 carrots, chopped
2 celery ribs, chopped
1 jalapeño pepper, seeded and chopped
1 cup dried mushrooms, reconstituted
1 tablespoon minced fresh ginger
1 medium butternut squash, peeled, seeded, and cubed
4 cups chicken broth
1 cup fat-free half-and-half
½ teaspoon salt
¼ teaspoon pepper

1. Heat oil in a Dutch oven.

2. Sauté leek, carrots, celery, jalapeño, mushrooms, and ginger in oil over medium heat for 10–15 minutes, or until tender.

3. Stir in butternut squash and chicken broth. Bring to a boil.

4. Reduce heat and simmer soup 30 minutes, or until squash is tender. Let cool slightly.

5. Puree soup in a food processor until smooth.

6. Return soup to Dutch oven and stir in half-and-half, salt, and pepper.

7. Cook over medium heat, stirring often, until heated through. Serve immediately.

SERVES 8–10

Egg Drop Soup with Mushrooms

2 cups chicken broth
¼ cup dried mushrooms, reconstituted
2 teaspoons lemon juice
2 teaspoons Kikkoman fried rice seasoning
1 egg, beaten and seasoned to taste
Yogurt, for garnish
Dill (preferably fresh) and/or finely sliced scallions, for garnish

1. Bring chicken broth, reconstituted mushrooms, lemon juice, and fried rice seasoning to a boil. Lower heat and simmer for about 5 minutes. (The recipe can be made up to this point in advance.)

2. When ready to serve the soup, bring it back to a boil and then slowly add the beaten egg, stirring constantly.

3. Divide the soup between two bowls and garnish with a dollop of yogurt, a sprig of dill, and scallions (if using).

SERVES 2

This soup lends itself well to experimentation with flavors, so try it with your favorite herbs and spices. I personally like dill, but ginger would be wonderful.

Bolete and Chicken Noodle Soup

> *6 cups chicken stock*
> *½ cup finely chopped celery*
> *1 tablespoon minced shallot or onion*
> *1 cup sliced bolete mushrooms (boletes are especially good but others may be substituted)*
> *2 ounces egg noodles*

1. Heat chicken stock in a large saucepan over medium-high heat.

2. Add celery and shallot and simmer for 2 minutes.

3. Add mushrooms and egg noodles and cook until tender.

SERVES 6

Dried and reconstituted boletes may be used in place of fresh mushrooms in this recipe, which serves as a wonderful foil to grilled cheese sandwiches on a cold winter day. All of the ingredients may be found in your pantry, especially if you use the boletes you found and dried last fall.

Pleurotus Chowder

½ *pound oyster mushrooms (*Pleurotus ostreatus*), chopped*
½ *cup finely chopped onion*
4 tablespoons butter or margarine
1 cup cubed potato
Salt and pepper to taste
Dash of mace
Pinch of chopped fresh chives
Dash of Tabasco sauce
¼ *teaspoon thyme*
2 cups milk
2 egg yolks, well beaten
¼ *cup sherry*
2 cups sour cream
Croutons, for garnish
Parsley, for garnish

1. Sauté mushrooms and onion in butter over medium-high heat until onion is translucent and mushrooms are tender.

2. Add potato cubes and cook over low heat until potato is tender, approximately 12–15 minutes.

3. Add salt and pepper, mace, chives, Tabasco, and thyme. Gradually stir in milk and bring to a boil.

4. Remove chowder from heat and gradually add egg yolks, sherry, and sour cream, one at a time. Return chowder to heat and bring to a boil.

5. Serve at once, garnished with croutons and parsley.

SERVES 4–5

Microwave Mushroom Soup

> 2 tablespoons butter or margarine
> ¾ cup chopped scallions
> 2 cups chopped mushrooms
> ¼ cup flour
> 3 teaspoons chicken bouillon granules
> Dash of pepper
> 1½ cups water
> 1½ cups milk

1. Combine butter, scallions, and mushrooms in a 2-quart casserole.

2. Microwave covered on high for 6 to 7 minutes, or until vegetables are tender, stirring once.

3. Stir in flour, bouillon granules, and pepper.

4. Gradually stir in water and milk.

5. Microwave uncovered on high for 10 to 15 minutes or until thickened, checking periodically.

YIELDS 4 CUPS

> Dried mushrooms—particularly morels, boletes, and shiitake—work well in place of fresh mushrooms in this recipe. If using shiitake, be sure to cut off the stems. They are tough and not very flavorful.

Asian Mushroom Noodle Soup

1 cup dried shiitake mushrooms
2 cups boiling water
1 cup chicken broth
1 cup julienned snow peas
½ cup diagonally-sliced scallions
2 teaspoons sesame oil
⅛ teaspoon pepper
2 cups cooked thin egg noodles
Salt to taste

1. Soak mushrooms in boiling water for 10 minutes. Strain liquid into a medium saucepan.

2. Add chicken broth and bring to a boil.

3. Cut stems from mushrooms (save for later use).

4. Cut mushroom caps diagonally into thin strips.

5. Add mushrooms, snow peas, scallions, sesame oil, and pepper to broth. Cook 1 minute, or until snow peas are crisp-tender.

6. Remove soup from heat. Add cooked noodles and add salt to taste.

SERVES 4

Creamy Onion Mushroom Soup

3 tablespoons butter or margarine
½ pound mushrooms, coarsely chopped
1 large onion, coarsely chopped
2 tablespoons flour
1 quart milk
3 chicken bouillon cubes or 3 teaspoons bouillon granules
¼ teaspoon thyme or dill weed

1. Melt butter in a large pan.

2. Sauté mushrooms and onion in butter over medium-high heat until limp.

3. Stir in flour. Remove from heat.

4. Gradually add milk. Then add bouillon and thyme or dill.

SERVES 6

For a delicious rainy day lunch, serve this soup with salad, biscuits, and cubes of sharp cheese. If it's extra rainy outside, try it with a nice slice of apple pie.

Curried Mushroom Turkey Soup

½ pound mushrooms, sliced
¼ cup chopped onion
4 tablespoons butter or margarine, melted
1 teaspoon curry powder
2 cups chicken broth
1½ cups water
1 cup diced potatoes
½ cup diced carrots
½ cups diagonally sliced celery
¼ teaspoon pepper
1½ cups diced cooked turkey
½ (10-ounce) package frozen French-style green beans
1 tablespoon chopped fresh parsley
½ teaspoon dried oregano
3 tablespoons flour
⅔ cup half-and-half

1. Sauté mushrooms and onion in butter in a Dutch oven over medium-high heat until onion is translucent and mushrooms are tender.

2. Stir in curry powder and cook for 2 minutes.

3. Add chicken broth, water, potatoes, carrots, celery, and pepper.

4. Bring to a boil, then reduce heat and simmer for 15 minutes.

5. Stir in turkey, green beans, parsley, and oregano. Continue simmering for 15 minutes more.

6. Meanwhile, combine flour and half-and-half and stir until smooth. Add the flour mixture to the soup and cook until thickened.

Serves 6–8

Corn and Shrimp Chowder with Mushrooms

1 tablespoon butter or margarine
1 tablespoon olive oil or vegetable oil
3 medium carrots, coarsely chopped
1 large onion, coarsely chopped
1 stalk celery, coarsely chopped
2 (10-ounce) packages frozen corn
1 (14.5-ounce) can chicken broth
2 teaspoons sugar
½ teaspoon salt
¼–½ teaspoon cayenne pepper
½ teaspoon dried thyme
2 cups water
½ cup half-and-half or light cream
1¾ pounds medium-size shrimp, peeled, deveined, and sliced

1. Melt butter with olive oil in a Dutch oven over medium heat. Heat until hot.

2. Add carrots, onion, and celery.

3. Cook about 15 minutes, or until vegetables are tender, stirring often.

4. Add corn (reserving 1½ cups), chicken broth, sugar, salt, cayenne pepper, thyme, and water to soup.

5. Bring to a boil, reduce heat to low, and simmer 20 minutes.

6. In a food processor, blend soup in small batches until smooth.

7. Return soup to pot. Add reserved corn.

8. Stir in half-and-half and heat soup over medium heat until hot.

9. Add sliced shrimp and cook for 5 minutes more.

SERVES 6–8

French Onion Soup with Mushrooms

2 cups sliced onions
½ pound mushrooms, sliced
1 stick (8 tablespoons) butter or margarine
1½ quarts beef stock
Salt and pepper to taste
4 slices French or Italian bread, toasted until dark
½ cup grated Parmesan cheese

1. Preheat oven to 400°F.

2. Sauté onions and mushrooms in 4 tablespoons butter until golden, stirring often.

3. Add beef stock, bring to a boil, and boil 10 minutes. Season soup to taste with salt and pepper.

4. Slather toast with the remaining butter and place in four small casserole dishes. Add soup and sprinkle with cheese.

5. Bake until the cheese topping is golden brown, watching carefully so the toast does not burn.

6. If desired, pass additional grated cheese after serving the soup.

Serves 4

This flavorsome soup is an excellent pairing for salad and good conversation. Have some friends over for lunch and see. What better excuse to try out that new dessert you've been itching to bake?

Shredded Chicken and Mushroom Soup

1 stick (8 tablespoons) butter or margarine
½ pound mushrooms, sliced
3 (14.5-ounce) cans chicken broth
2 large carrots, finely chopped
1 celery stalk, finely chopped
1 small onion, finely chopped
1 teaspoon finely chopped fresh parsley
Freshly grated nutmeg to taste
Pinch of salt
½–¾ cup shredded cooked chicken
2 eggs
2 tablespoons grated Parmesan cheese

1. Melt butter in a medium frying pan over medium heat.

2. Add mushrooms and cook until soft.

3. Put chicken broth, carrots, celery, onion, parsley, nutmeg, salt, chicken, and mushrooms in a Dutch oven over low heat and simmer 1½ hours. (Recipe can be made ahead up to this point.)

4. When ready to serve, beat eggs in a small bowl. Add cheese.

5. Bring soup to a rolling boil and whisk in egg mixture. Stir for 2 to 3 minutes. Serve at once.

SERVES 6–8

This soup is good with turkey as well as chicken. It is also a good way to use up leftovers, such as the rest of one of those roasted chickens from the deli.

Salads

Finnish Mushroom Salad

1 cup water
1 tablespoon lemon juice
½ pound mushrooms, thinly sliced
½ cup yogurt
2 tablespoons grated onion
Pinch of sugar
½ teaspoon salt
Dash of pepper
Lettuce

1. In a glass, enamel, or stainless pan over high heat, bring water and lemon juice to a boil.

2. Add mushrooms and cover.

3. Reduce heat and simmer gently for 3 minutes.

4. Remove pan from heat and drain mushrooms. Pat dry with a paper towel.

5. In a small bowl, combine yogurt, grated onion, sugar, salt, and pepper.

6. Add the mushrooms, and toss gently until well coated.

7. Serve mushrooms on crisp lettuce leaves.

SERVES 4

Note: Do not use aluminum pots or pans when making this dish. The lemon juice will stain them.

German Potato Salad

6 cups cubed redskin potatoes, boiled
1 small to medium onion, chopped
Salt and pepper to taste
6–8 strips bacon
⅓–½ pound mushrooms, sliced
⅓–½ cup red wine vinegar
⅛ cup sugar

1. Mix together potatoes, onion, and salt and pepper.

2. Cut bacon into small squares and fry until crisp. Remove from heat.

3. Fry mushrooms in bacon fat over medium-high heat until soft. Remove from heat.

4. Slowly pour vinegar over bacon and mushrooms. Add sugar and stir.

5. Pour bacon mixture over potato mixture and stir to blend thoroughly.

6. Let salad stand for 1 hour to let the flavors blend, then serve.

SERVES 8–10

Mushroom Bacon Salad

1 pound medium-size mushrooms
3 scallions, thinly sliced, including part of tops
⅓ cup olive oil or vegetable oil
4 tablespoons lemon juice
1 teaspoon Worcestershire sauce
½ teaspoon salt
½ teaspoon dry mustard
⅛ teaspoon pepper
12 slices bacon, cooked until crispy, crumbled
1 small head of lettuce, torn into bite-sized pieces

1. Slice mushrooms about ⅛ inch thick and place in a bowl.

2. Combine scallions, oil, lemon juice, Worcestershire sauce, salt, dry mustard, and pepper in a jar. Shake well and pour over mushrooms. Toss to mix well.

3. Cover mushrooms and refrigerate overnight (or at least 4 hours), stirring several times to ensure mushrooms are well coated with dressing.

4. Just before serving, add bacon to mushroom mixture. Toss mushroom mixture with lettuce and serve.

SERVES 6–8

Marinated Mushroom and Lemon Salad

1 pound mushrooms
Juice of 1 lemon
¾ cup safflower oil
¼ cup cider vinegar
2 garlic cloves, minced
¼ teaspoon pepper
1 teaspoon salt
1 lemon, cut into thin rounds
Fresh parsley, for serving

1. Cut stems from mushrooms (save for later use).

2. Place mushroom caps in a large saucepan and toss with lemon juice.

3. Add oil, vinegar, garlic, pepper, and salt and cook over medium-high heat for 20–30 minutes, stirring frequently.

4. Remove mushroom mixture from heat, cool to room temperature, and then chill at least one hour.

5. When ready to serve, drain marinade (save for later use).

6. Cover a serving plate with fresh parsley, place lemon rounds on top, spoon mushrooms over lemons, and serve.

SERVES 2

Mushroom Salad with No-Fat Mustard Dressing

1 cup buttermilk
½ cup Dijon mustard
Pepper to taste
6 ounces mushrooms, sliced
¾ pound fresh spinach
6 celery stalks

1. Combine buttermilk, mustard, and pepper in a jar. Shake well to thoroughly mix.

2. Combine mushrooms and ⅔ cup dressing in a large bowl, stirring to coat mushrooms. (Remaining dressing can be stored in refrigerator and used later; shake well before using.)

3. Tear spinach into bite-size pieces.

4. Cut celery stalks into ⅛-inch slices.

5. Just before serving, stir spinach and celery into mushroom mixture and toss well to coat.

SERVES 4

Hot Mushroom Salad

1 green pepper, sliced
1 small onion, sliced
1 pound mushrooms, sliced
1 tablespoon butter or margarine
1½ tablespoons soy sauce
1½ tablespoons teriyaki sauce
1 small head of lettuce, shredded
Crumbled bacon, for garnish

1. Combine green pepper, onion, mushrooms, butter, soy sauce, and teriyaki sauce in a skillet and cook over medium-high heat until tender.

2. Mix shredded lettuce with mushroom mixture in a bowl. Top with bacon and serve.

SERVES 4–6

Always cook morels before eating. Consuming raw morels will make you sick.

Mushrooms in Thyme Dressing

½ cup dry white wine
½ cup olive oil or vegetable oil
¼ cup lemon juice
2 garlic cloves, minced
1 teaspoon thyme
¼ teaspoon pepper
¾ teaspoon salt
2 teaspoons sugar
3 tablespoons chopped fresh parsley
1½ pounds small mushrooms (whole) or medium-size
   mushrooms (halved)
Lettuce for serving

1. Combine white wine, olive oil, lemon juice, garlic, thyme, pepper, salt, and sugar in a 3-quart saucepan. Add 2 tablespoons parsley.

2. Cover pan and simmer over low heat for 5 minutes. Add mushrooms, cover, and simmer 5 minutes more.

3. Refrigerate at least 4 hours or overnight.

4. Lift mushrooms from marinade with a slotted spoon and place in a lettuce-lined bowl. Garnish with remaining 1 tablespoon parsley.

SERVES 6

Marinated Mushroom Salad

½ cup vinegar
⅔ cup olive oil or vegetable oil
¼ cup chopped onion
2 garlic cloves, chopped
Salt and pepper to taste
1 teaspoon sugar
1 teaspoon dried basil
1 teaspoon dried oregano
2 cups sliced carrots, cooked
1 (14-ounce) can artichoke hearts
8 ounces mushrooms, halved
1 cup halved ripe olives
¼ cup chopped red pepper
Lettuce for serving

1. Combine vinegar, oil, onion, garlic, salt and pepper, sugar, basil, and oregano in a small saucepan.

2. Bring to a boil, then lower heat and simmer 10 minutes.

3. Put carrots, artichokes, mushrooms, olives, and red pepper in a large bowl.

4. Pour hot dressing over vegetables and cover.

5. Chill several hours, stirring several times.

6. Drain vegetables and serve over lettuce.

SERVES 6–8

Marinated Mushrooms and Avocados

¾ cup olive oil or vegetable oil

3 tablespoons white wine vinegar

3 tablespoons lemon juice

2 garlic cloves, minced

2 tablespoons chopped fresh parsley

1 teaspoon salt

1 teaspoon marjoram

1 teaspoon sugar

½ teaspoon dry mustard

½ teaspoon paprika

¼ teaspoon pepper

1 pound mushrooms, sliced

2 medium avocados

½ cup halved cherry tomatoes

1. Stir together oil, vinegar, lemon juice, garlic, parsley, salt, marjoram, sugar, dry mustard, paprika, and pepper, blending well.

2. Add sliced mushrooms and coat well with the marinade. Chill at least 3 hours.

3. About 1 hour before serving, peel, pit, and slice avocados and add to mushroom mixture, stirring to coat them with marinade.

4. Transfer salad to plates and garnish with cherry tomatoes.

SERVES 4–6

> Be sure to coat the avocados well with the marinade when you add them to the mixture. As in a fruit salad, the lemon juice will retard discoloration.

Mushroom, Chicken, and Vegetables Vinaigrette Salad

1 pound mushrooms, halved
Water (enough to cover the mushrooms)
1¼ cups chopped cooked chicken
1 pint cherry tomatoes, halved
2 small zucchini, sliced
1 green or red pepper, thinly sliced
1 green onion, thinly sliced (white and green parts)
½ cup olive oil or vegetable oil
2 tablespoons lemon juice
2 tablespoons white wine vinegar
1 teaspoon sugar
Salt and pepper to taste

1. Drop mushrooms into boiling water. Boil for 1 minute and drain.

2. Combine mushrooms, chicken, tomatoes, zucchini, green or red pepper, and green onion in a large bowl.

3. Combine oil, lemon juice, vinegar, sugar, and salt and pepper in a jar. Shake to mix well.

4. Pour dressing over chicken mixture, tossing gently.

5. Cover salad and chill several hours or overnight.

SERVES 6–8

Individual Stuffed Tomato Salads

6 medium tomatoes
4 slices of bacon
3 tablespoons olive oil or vegetable oil
1 tablespoon cider vinegar
2 teaspoons lemon juice
¼ teaspoon salt
¼ teaspoon dry mustard
¼ teaspoon oregano
⅛ teaspoon paprika
1 teaspoon minced fresh parsley
Dash of thyme
¼ pound mushrooms, thinly sliced
½ cup thinly sliced scallions
1 (9-ounce) package frozen Italian green beans, thawed and
   drained

1. Scoop out pulp from tomatoes and drain. Chill hollowed tomatoes until needed.

2. Cook bacon, crumble, and set aside.

3. Whisk together oil, vinegar, lemon juice, salt, mustard, oregano, paprika, parsley, and thyme in a large bowl. Let stand for several hours to blend flavors.

4. Stir mushrooms and scallions into dressing and chill 1–2 hours. Stir in green beans.

5. Stuff tomatoes with green bean mixture and garnish with crumbled bacon.

SERVES 6

Mushroom Relish

2 cups chicken broth
¾ cup dry white wine
½ cup olive oil or vegetable oil
¼ cup lemon juice
2 teaspoons salt
3 garlic cloves, halved
1 teaspoon thyme or dill weed
1½ pounds medium mushrooms (approximately 35)
1 small carrot, sliced
1 small green or red pepper, diced

1. In a large saucepan, bring broth, wine, oil, lemon juice, salt, garlic, and thyme or dill to a boil.

2. Reduce heat, cover, and simmer 15 minutes.

3. Add mushrooms to marinade, cover, and simmer 4 minutes.

4. Remove mushrooms with a slotted spoon and set aside.

5. Add carrot to marinade, cover, and simmer 3 minutes. Remove carrot with a slotted spoon and set aside.

6. Add green or red pepper to marinade, cover, and simmer 1 minute. Remove peppers with a slotted spoon and set aside.

7. Combine the vegetables, and divide them between two pint jars.

8. Pour enough marinade to cover vegetables into each jar, and then close tightly.

9. The vegetables can be served as a salad or relish. Use the remaining marinade as salad dressing. The relish will keep in the refrigerator for up to 3 weeks.

YIELDS 4 CUPS

Mushroom and Pepper Salad

1 medium red pepper
1 medium green pepper
¾ cup diagonally sliced celery
2 cups sliced mushrooms
¼ cup olive oil or vegetable oil
1 tablespoon plus 1 teaspoon red wine vinegar
1 tablespoon plus 1 teaspoon lemon juice
½ teaspoon sugar
2 medium Belgian endive heads
¼ cup sliced scallions

1. Slice the peppers into 1½ x ¼-inch strips.

2. Drop red peppers into boiling water for 45 seconds, then remove with a slotted spoon.

3. Repeat this process with green peppers, celery, and mushrooms.

4. Combine all the vegetables in a bowl and chill until needed.

5. Combine oil, vinegar, lemon juice, and sugar in a jar. Cover and shake well, and then chill until needed.

7. When ready to serve, combine vegetables and dressing, and mix well.

8. Arrange endive leaves on a large serving platter. Place vegetables on endive and garnish with scallions. Pour any remaining dressing over salad.

SERVES 8

Mushroom, Bacon, and Rice Salad

1 pound bacon
½ pound mushrooms, sliced
1 tablespoon lemon juice
3 cups cooked rice, chilled
¼ cup sliced radishes
¼ cup diced green pepper
¼ cup diced red pepper
¼ cup thinly sliced scallion
½ cup mayonnaise or salad dressing
Lettuce for serving
Minced fresh parsley, for garnish

1. Cook bacon until crispy. Crumble it.

2. Place mushrooms in boiling water for 1 minute, then remove from water and chill. Sprinkle lemon juice on mushrooms.

3. Combine bacon, mushrooms, rice, radishes, green and red pepper, and scallion in a large bowl. Mix thoroughly and toss with mayonnaise.

4. Serve salad on lettuce leaves and garnish with parsley.

SERVES 5–6

Some recipes call for mushroom caps rather than whole mushrooms, but those mushroom stems don't have to go to waste. Save unused mushroom stems for later use, such as adding savory flavor to broths or sauces.

Wild Mushroom Salad

1½ *ounces dried mushrooms*
1½ *pounds fresh button mushrooms*
¾ *cup olive oil or vegetable oil*
2 *tablespoons butter or margarine*
½ *teaspoon dill weed*
Salt and pepper to taste
½ *cup red wine vinegar*
8 *cups salad greens*

1. Place dried mushrooms in a small bowl and cover with boiling water. Soak for 1 hour, then drain and rinse well.

2. Remove stems from fresh mushrooms and slice the caps.

3. In a skillet over medium-high heat, sauté fresh mushrooms in 2 tablespoons olive oil and 2 tablespoons butter for 5 minutes.

4. Add dried mushrooms and dill, reduce heat to low, and cook for 5 minutes more.

5. Transfer mushrooms to a bowl.

6. Season with salt and pepper.

7. Add ¼ cup vinegar to skillet and bring to a boil. Deglaze skillet, scraping the pan to get all mushroom bits clinging to it. Pour hot vinegar mixture over mushrooms.

8. Combine remaining ¼ cup vinegar with remaining olive oil.

9. Toss greens with vinegar and oil mixture and spoon warm mushrooms on top.

SERVES 8

Green Bean and Mushroom Salad

1 tablespoon red wine vinegar
3 tablespoons olive oil or vegetable oil
½ cup minced scallions
1 teaspoon Dijon mustard
1 teaspoon finely chopped fresh dill
Salt and pepper to taste
½ pound mushrooms, quartered or sliced
1 pound green beans, sliced into 3-inch pieces
1 cup sour cream
Cherry tomatoes for garnish (optional)

1. Combine vinegar, oil, scallions, mustard, dill, and salt and pepper in a jar and shake well to blend.

2. Put mushrooms in boiling water and cook 3 minutes. Remove mushrooms from water, transfer to a bowl, and pour dressing over.

3. Put green beans in boiling water and cook until barely tender, approximately 8 minutes. Cool beans quickly by plunging them into ice water.

4. Add green beans to mushrooms. Add sour cream and mix thoroughly. Chill up to 4 hours.

5. Remove salad from refrigerator about 20 minutes before serving. Add additional seasoning if needed, and garnish with cherry tomatoes (if desired).

SERVES 4

Incredible Mushroom Salad

2 cups fresh spinach
4 ounces bacon, cut into matchsticks
¼ cup each shiitake, oyster, chanterelle, and portobello mushrooms,
  julienned
Salt and pepper to taste
1 hard-boiled egg, chopped
¼ cup Dijon mustard
1 egg yolk
2 tablespoons mayonnaise
1 cup olive oil or vegetable oil
¼ cup red wine vinegar
¼ cup honey
2 tablespoons sugar

1. Tear spinach into bite-size pieces and place in a salad bowl.

2. Sauté bacon over medium-high heat until brown and crispy. Set aside.

3. Add mushrooms to bacon grease and sauté over medium-high heat until tender.

4. Combine bacon and mushrooms and season with salt and pepper.

5. Spoon mushroom mixture over spinach and sprinkle with chopped egg.

6. Combine mustard, egg yolk, mayonnaise, and vinegar in a small bowl. Whisk for 2 or 3 minutes, slowly adding oil in a steady stream. Add honey and sugar, and season with salt and pepper.

7. Ladle dressing over salad.

SERVES 4–6

Overnight Salad

½ head lettuce
2 cups shredded carrots
5 scallions, thinly sliced (white and green parts)
14 slices bacon, cooked and crumbled
1 cup peas, cooked
½ cup thinly sliced mushrooms
2 tablespoons sugar
⅓ cup grated Parmesan cheese
1 cup mayonnaise
6 ounces shredded American cheese

1. Tear lettuce into bite-size pieces and mix with carrots.

2. Layer ingredients in a bowl in this order: lettuce mixture, scallions, crumbled bacon, peas, mushrooms, sugar, and Parmesan cheese.

3. Top salad with spoonfuls of mayonnaise.

4. Cover bowl tightly and refrigerate overnight. Toss just before serving, and fold in American cheese.

SERVES 4–6

This is a great salad to bring to potluck dinners and picnics. You can make it the day before, and it travels very well.

Pizza Rice Salad

1½ cups cooked rice
1 cup shredded mozzarella cheese
¾ cup sliced pepperoni, halved
1 large tomato, diced
2 cups sliced green peppers
2 cups sliced mushrooms
2 cups sliced ripe olives
2 cups sliced scallions
1 cup of your favorite Italian salad dressing

1. Toss rice with cheese, pepperoni, tomato, green peppers, mushrooms, olives, and scallions.

2. Add ½ cup salad dressing and toss again. Chill until ready to serve.

3. Just before serving, toss salad with the remaining dressing.

SERVES 6

This recipe is a great way to use leftover rice, and most of the ingredients will be found in your pantry. For an additional Italian accent, try serving it with homemade bread sticks dusted with Parmesan cheese and freshly baked.

Main Dishes: Beef

Egg Rolls

1 cup sour cream
¼ cup milk
3 tablespoons dry onion soup mix
2 tablespoons mustard
1 pound ground beef
1 small head of cabbage, finely chopped
½ green pepper, chopped
¼ pound mushrooms, finely chopped
4–5 scallions, chopped
2 eggs, scrambled
Salt and pepper to taste
Soy sauce to taste
Egg roll wrappers
Olive oil or vegetable oil

1. Make sauce by combining sour cream, milk, soup mix, and mustard in a saucepan. Warm over low heat until the mixture starts to bubble.

2. Brown ground beef in a skillet over medium-high heat until thoroughly cooked. Drain off fat.

3. Add cabbage, green pepper, mushrooms, scallions, and scrambled eggs to skillet. Cook until soft and heated through.

4. Season beef mixture with salt and pepper and soy sauce. Drain the mixture and chill up to thirty minutes.

5. Fill egg roll wrappers generously with beef mixture. Seal the edges by wetting with water and pressing firmly.

6. Brown in a small amount of oil. Serve with mustard sauce.

SERVES 8–10

Mushroom Meat Pie

4 tablespoons butter or margarine
1 medium onion, chopped
1½ pounds mushrooms, sliced
⅓ cup flour
1 cup cottage cheese
1 cup cubed cooked beef
⅓ cup chopped fresh parsley
1 teaspoon salt
¼ teaspoon pepper
¼ teaspoon rosemary
Pastry for double-crust pie (your recipe or premade)

1. Preheat oven to 425°F.

2. Melt butter in a frying pan over medium-high heat. Add onion and mushrooms and cook until liquid has mostly evaporated.

3. Stir in flour and cook until it begins to bubble. Remove mushroom mixture from heat.

4. Add cottage cheese, beef, parsley, salt, pepper, and rosemary to mushroom mixture.

5. Place pie crust in a 9-inch pie plate. Spoon in meat mixture.

6. Cover pie with top crust and make a slit in the top.

7. Bake pie for 45 minutes or until crust is golden brown.

8. Let stand for 15 minutes before cutting.

SERVES 6

This dish is usually made with beef, but it is also tasty with other meats. For a lighter pie, try substituting chicken or turkey.

London Broil Smothered in Wild Mushrooms

> *1 cup balsamic vinaigrette salad dressing*
> *¼ cup Dijon mustard*
> *2 garlic cloves, crushed*
> *2 teaspoons chopped fresh rosemary or dill*
> *1½- to 3-pound London broil, 2 inches thick*
> *2 tablespoons butter or margarine*
> *1 cup sliced white button mushrooms*
> *2 cups sliced shiitake mushrooms*
> *1 cup sliced portobello mushrooms*
> *½ cup minced shallots*
> *2 tablespoons Worcestershire sauce*
> *⅓ cup chopped fresh parsley*

1. In a plastic food storage bag, combine dressing, mustard, garlic, and rosemary or dill.

2. Add steak to bag.

3. Seal bag, turning to coat the meat, and refrigerate for 24 hours, turning a few times.

4. Preheat broiler. Place broiler rack so that the top of the meat will be 4 inches from heat source. Coat broiler rack with cooking spray.

5. Remove steak from bag, reserving marinade.

6. Place steak on pan and broil for 8 to 10 minutes per side (for medium-rare).

7. Transfer meat to serving platter. Let stand for 5 minutes.

8. Meanwhile, in a nonstick frying pan, melt butter over medium heat.

9. Add mushrooms and shallots and cook until softened, 3 to 4 minutes.

10. Add Worcestershire sauce, parsley, and reserved marinade.

11. Cook until thickened, 2 to 3 minutes.

12. Pour mushroom mixture over steak.

SERVES 8–10

London broil is found in the meat section of just about every grocery store. It is wonderful for parties, holiday gatherings, weddings, and any other celebrations. If you have a large gathering, purchase two or three pieces of meat and cook each one differently. Make one rare, one medium, and one well done. This way, everyone has meat cooked to their preference.

Round Steak Stroganoff

½ cup flour
1 teaspoon salt
½ teaspoon pepper
1 teaspoon paprika
1½–2 pounds round steak, cut into thin strips
3 tablespoons butter or margarine
1 cup chopped onion
1 garlic clove, minced
1 (10.5-ounce) can condensed beef broth
½ teaspoon dry mustard
3 tablespoons chili sauce
1 pound mushrooms, sliced
2 cups sour cream
1 package egg noodles, cooked
Fresh parsley, for garnish

1. Combine flour, salt, pepper, and paprika in a plastic food storage bag. Shake beef strips in bag until well coated.

2. In a large skillet, melt butter over medium heat.

3. Brown half of the beef at a time. Remove from skillet and set aside.

4. Add onion and garlic to skillet, and cook over medium-high heat until tender.

5. Return beef to skillet and add broth, mustard, chili sauce, and mushrooms.

6. Cover and simmer until the beef is tender, about 1 hour.

7. Just before serving, stir in sour cream. Heat stroganoff gently but do not boil. Serve immediately over noodles, garnished with chopped parsley.

SERVES 6–8

Beef and Broccoli Squares

1 (10-ounce) package frozen chopped broccoli
1 pound ground beef
¼ pound mushrooms, sliced
2 cups shredded cheddar cheese
½ cup chopped onion
2 cups Bisquick baking mix
½ cup cold water
¼ cup Parmesan cheese
1 teaspoon salt
Dash of pepper
¼ cup milk
4 eggs

1. Preheat oven to 400°F. Grease a 12 x 7½ x 1¾-inch baking dish.

2. Thaw and drain broccoli.

3. Cook beef in 10-inch skillet over medium-high heat, stirring until brown. Drain.

4. Stir in mushrooms, 1½ cups cheddar cheese, and onion.

5. In a bowl, combine baking mix, water, and remaining ½ cup cheddar cheese. Beat until a soft dough forms.

6. Pat dough into prepared baking dish with floured hands, pressing it ½ inch up sides.

7. Spread beef mixture over dough. Sprinkle with broccoli.

8. Mix together Parmesan cheese, salt, pepper, milk, and eggs. Pour over broccoli.

9. Bake until knife inserted near center comes out clean, 25 to 30 minutes.

SERVES 6–8

Asian Beef Supper

1 pound ground beef
1 (10-ounce) can undiluted cream of mushroom soup
1 (16-ounce) can bean sprouts, drained
1 (8-ounce) can water chestnuts, drained
¼–½ pound mushrooms, sliced
½–¾ cup water
1 cup diced celery
½ cup uncooked instant rice
2 tablespoons instant minced onion
½ teaspoon salt
¼ teaspoon pepper
1 (3-ounce) can chow mein noodles

1. Cook beef in a skillet over medium-high heat until browned, stirring to crumble. Drain off pan drippings.

2. Add soup, bean sprouts, water chestnuts, mushrooms, water, celery, rice, onion, salt, and pepper. Simmer 20 minutes.

3. Spoon mixture into a serving dish and sprinkle with noodles.

SERVES 6–8

Beef Bourguignon

3 pounds lean beef chuck, cut into cubes
¼ cup oil
3 tablespoons flour
1½ teaspoons salt
½ teaspoon pepper
½ teaspoon dried thyme
1 (10.75-ounce) can condensed beef broth
1 cup red wine (plus more if needed)
½ pound mushrooms, quartered
12 small white onions

1. Preheat oven to 325°F.

2. In a skillet, sauté meat in oil over medium-high heat until brown.

3. Stir in flour, salt, pepper, and thyme to coat the meat. Scrape bottom of skillet well and turn all into a 2-quart casserole. Pour on beef broth and wine.

4. Bake for 2 hours.

5. Add mushrooms and onions.

6. Add equal amounts of water and wine if the mixture seems dry.

7. Continue baking for 1 to 1½ hours longer.

8. Serve with rice, mashed potatoes, or noodles.

SERVES 8

Beef Teriyaki

⅓ *cup dry sherry*
½ *cup chicken broth*
½ *cup soy sauce*
1 garlic clove, minced
1 teaspoon sugar
1 (1½-pound) flank steak
1 tablespoon olive oil or vegetable oil
1 medium-size sweet potato, peeled and thinly sliced
12 small mushrooms, halved
1 green pepper, cut into 1-inch pieces
4 scallions, cut into 1-inch pieces
1 cup fresh bean sprouts
Cooked rice

1. To make marinade, combine sherry, broth, soy sauce, garlic, and sugar. Reserve ⅓ cup marinade for later use. Pour the rest into plastic food storage bag.

2. Marinate steak in plastic food storage bag for 15 minutes.

3. Drain steak and pat dry. Preheat broiler.

4. Broil steak 4 inches from heat, 2 or 3 minutes on each side.

5. Heat oil in a wok or skillet.

6. Add sweet potato slices and fry for 1 minute over high heat.

7. Add mushrooms, green peppers, and scallions.

8. Fry for 2 to 3 minutes, until crisp-tender.

9. Stir sprouts into the vegetables and place on a heated platter.

10. Serve the steak sliced with the vegetables, reserved marinade, and rice.

SERVES 6

Stir-Fry Beef over Warm Greens

¾ pound beef sirloin
1 (8-ounce) bottle oil-and-vinegar salad dressing
2 tablespoons each dry sherry and soy sauce
1 tablespoon brown sugar
½ teaspoon minced garlic
⅛ teaspoon ground ginger
12 cups torn mixed greens
1½ cups sliced shiitake caps
½ cup sliced scallions
1 tablespoon olive oil or vegetable oil
1 large red pepper, cut into thin strips

1. Trim fat from meat and cut into bite-size pieces. Let rest in freezer until partially frozen.

2. To make marinade, combine salad dressing, sherry, soy sauce, brown sugar, garlic, and ginger in a plastic food storage bag.

3. Marinate meat for at least 6 hours or overnight, turning frequently.

4. In a large bowl, toss greens, mushrooms, and scallions.

5. Divide among 6 dinner plates.

6. Remove meat from marinade, reserving ⅔ cups marinade.

7. Heat a large skillet or wok over high heat, then add oil.

8. Stir-fry meat for 2 or 3 minutes, until tender.

9. Add pepper strips and fry for 2 minutes, until crisp-tender.

10. Add reserved marinade and heat thoroughly.

11. Spoon meat mixture over greens and serve immediately.

SERVES 6

Truffle Roast Beef Tenderloin with Sherry Cream and Morel Sauce

3 tablespoons white truffle oil
2 tablespoons kosher salt
1 tablespoon pepper
2 tablespoons minced garlic
2 tablespoons thyme
2 tablespoons rosemary
2-pound beef tenderloin, trimmed and tied
2 tablespoons butter or margarine
2 tablespoons olive oil or vegetable oil
1 tablespoon minced garlic
1 cup finely julienned leeks (2-inch strips)
Scant ¼ cup cream sherry
¼ cup bordelaise sauce (see recipe page 131)
⅛ cup heavy cream
12 dried morel mushrooms, rehydrated

1. Preheat oven to 425°F.

2. Mix together truffle oil, salt and pepper, garlic, thyme, and rosemary. Rub generously onto meat.

3. Place meat in oven and roast until meat reaches an internal temperature of 135°F for medium-rare.

4. Remove meat from the oven and let rest for 8–14 minutes before slicing.

5. Meanwhile, to make the sauce, heat butter and oil in a medium frying pan over high heat.

6. Lightly brown garlic. Add leeks and remove from heat.

7. Add sherry. Return sauce to medium heat and add bordelaise sauce, cream, and mushrooms.

8. Simmer sauce, stirring constantly, and reduce to desired consistency.

9. Season sauce with salt and pepper to taste. Serve immediately with tenderloin.

SERVES 4

Bordelaise Sauce
2 tablespoons butter
1 shallot, chopped fine
1 slice onion
2 slices carrot
Parsley
½ bay leaf
8 peppercorns
1 clove
1 cup consommé

Sauté vegetables and seasonings in butter until well browned. Add consommé, simmer 8 minutes, and strain.

Truffles are found growing wild in Europe. In the United States, they are grown commercially. They have a very strong flavor, so only very thin slices are needed in most dishes. In fact, it takes only one small truffle to flavor an entire 10-pound bag of rice.

Main Dishes: Pork

Ham and Shrimp Curry

¼ *cup chopped onion*
¼ *cup chopped celery*
4 tablespoons butter or margarine, melted
¼ *cup flour*
1–2 teaspoons curry powder
¼ *teaspoon salt*
Dash of pepper
2 cups milk
½ *cup sliced mushrooms*
1½ *cups diced cooked ham*
1 pound cleaned cooked shrimp

1. Cook onion and celery in butter in a large saucepan over medium-high heat until transparent.

2. Blend in flour, curry powder, salt, and pepper.

3. Heat until the mixture begins to bubble.

4. Gradually add milk, stirring constantly, and cook until thick.

5. Add mushrooms, ham, and shrimp and heat until warmed through.

6. Serve with rice and condiments for curry (see list page 133).

SERVES 8–10

Note: This recipe can be doubled and tripled for large groups. It tastes better the longer it sits, so consider making it in the morning and reheating it just before serving.

**Recommended curry condiments
(1 cup each):**

Finely chopped cashews or peanuts

Crushed pineapple

Coconut

Crumbled crisp bacon

Finely chopped cucumber

Diced banana

Finely chopped hard-boiled eggs

Finely chopped scallions (white and
green parts)

Finely chopped green pepper

Chopped fresh tomatoes

Lime wedges (to squeeze on top)

Chutney

Ham and Cheese Strata

> 6 cups cubed day-old French bread
> 1½ cups milk
> 2 tablespoons butter or margarine
> 1 onion, chopped
> 1 garlic clove, minced
> 10 ounces mushrooms, sliced
> ½ teaspoon herbes de Provence
> ½ teaspoon salt
> ½ teaspoon pepper
> 1 package baby spinach leaves
> 1½ cups chopped ham
> 1¼ cups shredded Jarlsberg cheese
> 1 cup cream
> 4 eggs

1. Butter a 2-quart baking dish.

2. In a bowl, combine bread cubes and milk.

3. Let stand until milk is absorbed, about 10 minutes.

4. In a nonstick skillet, melt butter over medium heat.

5. Add onion and garlic, and cook until softened, about 4 minutes.

6. Stir in mushrooms.

7. Cook until liquid is almost evaporated, about 7 minutes.

8. Stir in herbes de Provence, ¼ teaspoon salt, and ¼ teaspoon pepper.

9. Add spinach.

10. Cook, stirring often, until wilted. Remove spinach-mushroom mixture from heat.

11. Arrange half of bread cubes in bottom of baking dish.

12. Top with spinach-mushroom mixture.

13. Sprinkle with chopped ham and then 1 cup cheese.

14. Top with remaining bread cubes and sprinkle with remaining ¼ cup cheese.

15. In a bowl, whisk together cream, eggs, remaining ¼ teaspoon salt, and remaining ¼ teaspoon pepper. Pour over strata.

16. Cover strata and refrigerate for at least 1½ hours.

17. Preheat oven to 350°F. Bake strata until golden brown, about 50 minutes.

SERVES 8

> Herbes de Provence may be found in fine grocery stores or specialty gourmet shops.

Sweet and Sour Pork with Mushrooms

1½ pounds lean pork, cut into 2 x ½-inch strips
⅓ cup olive oil or vegetable oil
½ cup water
2½ cups canned pineapple chunks, including syrup
¼ cup brown sugar
2 tablespoons cornstarch
¼ cup cider vinegar
2–3 tablespoons soy sauce
Salt to taste
1 small green pepper, cut into strips
¼ cup thinly sliced onion
½ pound mushrooms, thinly sliced

1. Brown pork in hot oil in a large skillet over high heat until browned on all sides.

2. Add water, then cover and simmer until pork is tender, about 1 hour.

3. Drain pineapple, reserving syrup. Set pineapple chunks aside.

4. Combine sugar and cornstarch.

5. Add pineapple syrup, vinegar, soy sauce, and salt.

6. Add sugar mixture to pork, and cook, stirring, until gravy thickens.

7. Add pineapple, green pepper, onion, and mushrooms.

8. Cook 3–4 minutes.

9. Serve over rice.

SERVES 6–8

Pork Chops with Mushroom Sauce

¼ cup plus 2 tablespoons flour, divided
¾ teaspoon dried thyme
¾ teaspoon dried marjoram
¾ teaspoon salt
¾ teaspoon pepper
6 rib pork chops (1 inch thick; about 3 pounds)
1 tablespoon plus 1 teaspoon olive oil or vegetable oil
½ cup chicken broth
¼ pound mushrooms, sliced
¼ cup chopped onion
⅓ cup Marsala wine

1. Combine ¼ cup flour, thyme, marjoram, salt, and pepper.

2. Coat both sides of chops with flour mixture.

3. In a large skillet, heat oil over medium-high heat.

4. Add chops and cook until browned, about 6 minutes per side.

5. Reduce heat to medium and cook chops until almost done, 2 to 3 minutes per side.

6. Transfer chops to a platter and keep warm.

7. Combine broth with remaining 2 tablespoons flour and set aside.

8. In same skillet used for the chops, over medium-high heat, cook mushrooms and onion until tender, about 3 to 4 minutes.

9. Add wine and deglaze the pan, scraping up any browned bits.

10. Add broth mixture and cook until mixture thickens, about 3 minutes.

11. Return chops to skillet with sauce and heat through, about 1 to 2 minutes.

SERVES 6

Ham and Mushroom Pizza

Pastry for single-crust pie (your recipe or premade)
½ teaspoon poppy seeds
½ pound mushrooms, sliced
⅓ cup chopped onion
2 tablespoons butter or margarine
¼ pound cooked ham, sliced
½ pound Swiss cheese, sliced
3 eggs
¾ cup milk

1. Preheat oven to 425°F.

2. Prepare pastry, adding poppy seeds with the dry ingredients or working into prepared dough.

3. Roll out pastry and fit into a 12-inch pizza pan. Crimp sides.

4. Bake pastry on lowest oven rack for 5 minutes. Meanwhile, sauté mushrooms and onion in butter in a medium-size skillet over medium-high heat until limp.

5. Remove pastry from oven, press out bubbles, and top with ham and cheese.

6. Spread mushrooms and onion over ham and cheese.

7. Beat together eggs and milk and pour over pizza.

8. Return pizza to lowest oven rack and bake 18 to 20 minutes more, or until eggs have set.

SERVES 4

Pork and Mushroom Kabobs

½ cup soy sauce
2 tablespoons brown sugar
2 tablespoons lemon juice
1½ teaspoons salt
1 teaspoon ginger
1 teaspoon coriander
1 teaspoon cumin
1 large onion, thinly sliced
1 garlic clove, minced
1 cup olive oil or vegetable oil
2½ pounds pork, cut into 1- to 1½-inch cubes
20 medium-size mushrooms
½ cup finely chopped salted peanuts

1. In a bowl, combine soy sauce, brown sugar, lemon juice, salt, ginger, coriander, cumin, onion, and garlic.

2. Add oil and stir until blended.

3. Add pork and stir until well coated.

4. Cover and marinate in refrigerator several hours or overnight.

5. Reserve marinade. Alternate pork cubes with mushrooms on 6 skewers.

7. Roll kabobs in peanuts.

8. Preheat broiler. Arrange kabobs on a broiler pan and set about 4 inches from heat.

9. Broil kabobs, turning and basting carefully several times with marinade, for about 15 minutes. Cut into one cube to test for doneness.

SERVES 6

Date-Stuffed Pork Tenderloin with Mushrooms

4 tablespoons butter or margarine, melted
1 cup finely chopped pitted dates
2 cups small cubes white bread
½ teaspoon salt
½ teaspoon sage
2 (10-ounce) cans cream of celery or mushroom soup
2 (1½ pounds each) whole pork tenderloins
1 teaspoon garlic salt
½ pound mushrooms, sliced
1½ cup water
½ cup white wine

1. Preheat oven to 350°F.

2. Combine butter, dates, bread, salt, and sage, and cover.

3. Microwave on high for 4 minutes. Stir in 1 cup of soup.

4. Split tenderloins lengthwise, almost all the way through, and lay them flat. Make a shallow slit lengthwise in the center of each half.

5. Sprinkle inside surface of tenderloins with garlic salt.

6. Spread half of date mixture on half of each tenderloin.

7. Fold halves of each tenderloin together, forming two separate stuffed roasts.

8. Tie each in three places with string.

9. Place tenderloins in shallow baking pan.

10. Spread remaining soup over the roasts and spread sliced mushrooms over all.

11. Bake for 1¼ hours, or until tender.

12. Let stand for 10 minutes.

13. Remove string, and then slice.

14. Serve tenderloin topped with pan drippings diluted to taste. (To dilute, use 3 parts water to 1 part white wine, brought to a simmer.)

15. Divide mushrooms among the servings.

SERVES 8

Main Dishes: Lamb

Arabian Meat Pies

1/4 cup olive oil or vegetable oil
2 sticks (16 tablespoons) butter or margarine
1/2 cup warm water
1 teaspoon salt
2 cups flour
1 pound ground lamb
1 medium onion, chopped
1/2 cup minced mushrooms
2 tablespoons olive oil or butter
1 teaspoon pepper
Salt to taste
2 tablespoons pine nuts
3–4 tablespoons chopped fresh parsley

1. Preheat oven to 350°F.

2. Put oil and butter in bowl. Mix in water and salt.

3. Gradually add flour, stirring slowly with hands until it forms a soft ball. Handle as little as possible.

4. Roll dough out thinly, and cut into 4-inch rounds.

5. For filling, mix together lamb, onion, mushrooms, oil, pepper, salt, pine nuts, and parsley.

6. Put 1 large tablespoon filling in the center of each round.

7. Fold each in half, moisten edges with water, and press edges closed with tines of a fork.

8. Bake pies until golden brown.

SERVES 8–10

Mushroom-Stuffed Lamb Loaves

1 tablespoon butter or margarine
1 tablespoon olive oil or vegetable oil
½ cup finely chopped onion
1 cup fine bread crumbs
½ cup chopped fresh parsley
1½ cups chopped mushrooms
1¼ cups water
2 pounds ground lamb
½ teaspoon dried mint
½ teaspoon coriander
½ teaspoon salt
¼ teaspoon pepper

1. Preheat oven to 350°F.

2. In a large skillet, heat butter and oil. Add onion, bread crumbs, parsley, and mushrooms.

3. Stir over heat for 2 to 3 minutes to thoroughly mix.

4. Add water to moisten stuffing evenly.

5. Cover and cook 1 minute, and then remove from heat. Set stuffing aside.

6. Mix lamb with mint, coriander, salt, and pepper.

7. Shape into 12 thin, round patties.

8. Spoon stuffing evenly onto 6 patties. Top each with another patty.

9. Crimp edges of patties together to form small, rounded loaves.

10. Place loaves in shallow baking pan.

11. Bake loaves for 30 minutes, or until cooked through.

Serves 6

Lamb Curry

2 garlic cloves, minced
4 large onions, minced
12 tablespoons butter or margarine
3 pounds lamb, cut into cubes
¼ cup flour
4 medium apples, peeled and chopped
4 tablespoons curry powder (or more to taste)
4 tablespoons brown sugar
4 tablespoons raisins
2 tablespoons Worcestershire sauce
2 lemons, peeled, seeded, and diced
4 tablespoons coconut
¾ cup chopped walnuts or almonds
½ teaspoon grated lime peel
1 tablespoon salt
2 cups water
½ cup mushrooms

1. Sauté garlic and onions in butter for 5 minutes.

2. Dust lamb with flour, add to garlic and onions, and sauté for 10 minutes more, stirring constantly.

3. Add apples and curry powder to pan and simmer 5 minutes.

4. Mix in brown sugar, raisins, Worcestershire sauce, lemons, coconut, walnuts, lime peel, and salt.

5. Add water and bring curry to a boil. Reduce heat and cover; simmer for 1 hour.

6. Add mushrooms 10 minutes before serving curry.

7. Serve curry on Chinese noodles or rice.

8. Accompany with curry condiments (see below).

SERVES 12

**Recommended curry condiments
(1 cup each):**
Chunks of fresh coconut
Chutney
Candied kumquats
Candied watermelon rind

Roast Lamb with Mushrooms

> *1 leg of lamb, boned and rolled (ask your butcher to do this for you)*
> *1 garlic clove*
> *Juice of 1 lemon*
> *½ teaspoon dry mustard*
> *½ teaspoon curry powder*
> *½ teaspoon butter or margarine*
> *½ teaspoon salt*
> *½ teaspoon pepper*
> *½ pound mushrooms, sliced*
> *1 cup burgundy wine*
> *3 tablespoons black or red currant jelly*

1. Place lamb in a roasting pan.

2. Mix together garlic, lemon juice, dry mustard, curry powder, and butter.

3. Rub the lamb with the spice mix.

4. Let stand for at least 3 hours in the refrigerator.

5. Add salt, pepper, and mushrooms to roasting pan.

6. Preheat oven to 325°F.

7. Roast lamb for 30 minutes per pound.

8. In a small saucepan, heat wine and jelly together. Baste lamb at least 3 times with the wine and jelly mixture while roasting.

9. Spoon off excess fat from roasting pan ½ hour before meat is cooked. Serve lamb with mushrooms over the top.

10. Use pan juices to make gravy by heating over high heat until bubbly. While heating, stir in flour to thicken.

SERVES 8

Lamb Chops with Mushrooms and Herbs

6 lamb chops, boned and rolled (ask your butcher to do this for you)
Salt and pepper to taste
2 tablespoons butter or margarine
1 teaspoon tarragon
¼ pound mushrooms, chopped (reserve 3 mushroom caps)
2 teaspoons tarragon vinegar
2 tablespoons tomato sauce
6 tablespoons cream
3 English muffins, split, toasted, and buttered

1. Sprinkle chops with salt and pepper.

2. Melt butter in frying pan.

3. Add tarragon and chops, and brown meat on all sides, cooking until it is done as you wish.

4. Remove meat from pan and keep warm.

5. Slightly brown 3 whole mushroom caps in remaining butter. Set aside with the meat.

6. Add chopped mushrooms to frying pan.

7. Cook over high heat for about 2 minutes, stirring all the time.

8. Mix in vinegar, tomato sauce, and cream and cook until sauce has thickened, approximately 5 to 10 minutes.

9. To serve, place 2 chops on each of 3 muffin halves. Pour the sauce over each and top each sandwich with one of the mushroom caps. Cut remaining 3 muffin halves in quarters and serve alongside.

SERVES 3

Special Lamb Chops

6 shoulder or loin lamb chops, ½ inch thick
Butter or margarine
Salt and pepper to taste
1 (10.5-ounce) can condensed consommé
½ teaspoon dried thyme
½ cup chopped celery
½ cup sliced scallions, reserve tops
½ cup sliced mushrooms
3 tablespoons flour
1 tablespoon parsley
1 cup sour cream

1. Slowly brown chops in a small amount of butter in a large skillet over medium-high heat.

2. Season with salt and pepper. Drain off fat.

3. Add consommé, thyme, celery, scallions, and mushrooms to pan.

4. Simmer covered for 30 to 45 minutes. Remove chops.

5. Stir flour, blended with a small amount of water, into pan. Cook, stirring, until thickened.

6. Return chops to pan and add parsley.

7. Top each chop with sour cream.

8. Heat covered for 3 minutes.

9. Sprinkle with chopped scallion tops.

SERVES 4–6

Main Dishes: Chicken

Greek Chicken Breasts with Mushrooms

4 chicken breasts, bone-in
2 tablespoons olive oil or vegetable oil
1 teaspoon salt
1 teaspoon black pepper
1 teaspoon garlic powder
2 teaspoons dried oregano
4 lemons, thinly sliced
16–20 pitted kalamata olives
¼ pound mushrooms, sliced
¼ pound feta cheese, crumbled

1. Preheat oven to 350°F.

2. Rub chicken evenly with oil.

3. Sprinkle with salt, pepper, garlic powder, and oregano.

4. Place lemon slices in a 9 x 13-inch baking pan.

5. Arrange chicken breasts over lemons.

6. Sprinkle olives and mushrooms around the chicken.

7. Bake for 45 minutes.

8. Remove chicken from oven and sprinkle with feta cheese.

SERVES 4

Curried Chicken and Couscous Pilaf

3 cups frozen vegetable mix (including broccoli, red peppers, onions, and mushrooms)
¼ cup wild mushrooms
5 tablespoons butter or margarine, melted
1 teaspoon minced garlic
1⅓ cups chicken broth
1 teaspoon curry powder
¼ teaspoon pepper
⅛ teaspoon cayenne pepper (optional)
1 cup uncooked couscous
½ cup chopped dried fruit, such as Sunsweet Fruit Morsels
1 (2½-pound) rotisserie chicken, quartered

1. Place vegetables in a microwave-safe bowl and cover.

2. Microwave on high, stirring occasionally, until heated through, about 6 minutes. Set aside.

3. Meanwhile, in a large saucepan, heat 4 tablespoons butter over medium heat.

4. Add garlic and cook for 1 minute.

5. Add broth, ¾ teaspoon curry powder, pepper, and cayenne.

6. Bring to a boil. Stir in vegetables, couscous, and dried fruit.

7. Cover and remove from heat. Let stand for 5 minutes.

8. Meanwhile, combine remaining 1 tablespoon butter and ¼ teaspoon curry powder.

9. Brush over chicken.

10. Fluff couscous with a fork and transfer to a platter.

11. Top couscous with the chicken and serve.

SERVES 4

Ginger Chicken and Mushrooms

3 tablespoons lemon juice
3 tablespoons soy sauce
1 tablespoon grated fresh ginger
2 garlic cloves, finely minced
2 skinless boneless chicken breast halves, cut into ½-inch strips
2 tablespoons cornstarch
⅓ cup chicken broth
2 tablespoons olive oil or vegetable oil
½ pound mushrooms, quartered
1 pound asparagus, sliced into 1½-inch pieces
3 scallions, sliced diagonally into 1-inch pieces
Toasted sesame seeds, for garnish
Lemon slices, for garnish
Fresh cilantro or parsley, for garnish

1. Combine lemon juice, soy sauce, ginger, and garlic.

2. Toss liquid with chicken to coast evenly. Set aside.

3. Mix cornstarch and chicken broth, set aside.

4. In a skillet, heat oil to sizzling. Drain chicken, reserving liquid.

5. Add mushrooms and drained chicken to skillet.

6. Cook until chicken loses its pink color.

7. Add asparagus and scallions.

8. Continue to toss over high heat until vegetables are crisp-tender.

9. Add cornstarch mixture and stir until thickened.

10. Sprinkle chicken with sesame seeds.

11. Serve over hot rice, garnished with lemon slices and cilantro or parsley.

SERVES 4

Hot Chicken Cobbler

> 6 tablespoons butter, melted
> 4 cups cubed sourdough rolls
> 1/3 cup grated Parmesan cheese
> 2 tablespoons chopped fresh parsley
> 2 medium-size sweet onions, sliced
> 1/2 pound mushrooms, sliced
> 1 cup white wine or buttermilk
> 1 (10.75-ounce) can cream of mushroom soup
> 1/2 cup roasted red bell peppers, drained and chopped
> 2 1/2 cups shredded cooked chicken

1. Preheat oven to 400°F. Lightly grease a 9-inch square or 11 x 7-inch baking dish.

2. Toss 4 teaspoons melted butter with sourdough rolls, Parmesan cheese, and parsley. Set aside.

3. Sauté onions in remaining 2 tablespoons butter in a large skillet over medium-high heat.

4. Cook for 15 minutes, or until golden brown.

5. Add mushrooms and sauté 5 minutes.

6. Stir in wine, soup, red peppers, and chicken.

7. Cook, stirring constantly, for 5 minutes, or until bubbly.

8. Spoon mushroom-chicken mixture into prepared baking dish.

9. Top evenly with bread mixture.

10. Bake for 15 minutes, or until cobbler is golden brown.

SERVES 4

Chicken and Chanterelles

2 chicken breasts, skin and bones removed (reserve bones), julienned
2 celery stalks, sliced
2 carrots, sliced
3 cups water
3 tablespoons minced shallots
3 tablespoons butter or margarine
1 pound fresh chanterelles, cut into small pieces
¼ cup dry vermouth
⅓ cup cream
Salt and pepper to taste
Chopped fresh parsley, for garnish

1. Combine chicken bones, celery, carrots, and water. Bring to a boil.

2. Simmer mixture, skimming froth, for 1 hour.

3. Reduce chicken stock over high heat to about 1 cup. Strain and set aside.

4. Cook shallots in butter over medium heat for 2 minutes, or until softened.

5. Add chanterelles and toss to coat with butter.

6. Add chicken stock and cook until liquid is reduced by half.

7. Add vermouth and reduce liquid to about 2 tablespoons.

8. Add cream and salt and pepper. Cook until sauce is thickened.

9. Stir in chicken pieces and cook until chicken is just cooked through.

10. Transfer the mixture to a heated serving dish.

11. Sprinkle with parsley.

SERVES 4

Individual Chicken Wellingtons

3 shallots
½ pound mushrooms
2 tablespoons butter or margarine
½ cup diced red pepper
½ teaspoon dried thyme
¾ teaspoon salt
¼ teaspoon pepper
¼ cup chopped fresh parsley
1 (17.25-ounce) package frozen puff pastry, thawed
6 skinless boneless chicken breast halves
2 tablespoons Dijon mustard
¼ cup bread crumbs
1 egg, lightly beaten

1. Preheat oven to 425°F.

2. Finely chop shallots and mushrooms.

3. In a skillet, melt butter over medium-high heat.

4. Add shallots, mushrooms, red pepper, thyme, ½ teaspoon salt, and ⅛ teaspoon pepper.

5. Cook, stirring often, until liquid evaporates.

6. Remove mushroom mixture from heat and add parsley.

7. Unfold pastry dough on a floured surface.

8. Roll out each sheet to a 14 x 12-inch rectangle and cut each rectangle into 4 pieces.

9. Sprinkle chicken with remaining ¼ teaspoon salt and ⅛ teaspoon pepper.

10. Spread 1 teaspoon of mustard in an oval from corner to corner of each of 6 pastry rectangles.

11. Spread ¼ cup mushroom mixture over the mustard on each pastry rectangle.

12. Place 1 piece of chicken on a rectangle, tucking under edges to fit within the mushroom mixture.

13. Sprinkle chicken with 2 teaspoons of bread crumbs.

14. Brush pastry edges with egg, fold dough over chicken, and pinch edges to seal.

15. Place packet seam side down on a jelly roll pan.

16. Repeat with the 5 other chicken breasts.

17. Brush each packet with egg.

18. Bake packets until golden and cooked through, about 20 minutes.

19. Serve with asparagus, green beans, or your favorite vegetable.

SERVES 6

> Incorporating mushrooms into your family's meals could be good for their health. Each year more research is carried out on the nutritional value of mushrooms. It seems that each issue of the common women's magazines has references to some new study. Recently, one study purportedly found that a large portobello mushroom can provide close to 400 IU of vitamin D. Another stated that people who each mushrooms have stronger bones than those who do not eat mushrooms.

Chicken Florentine with Mushroom Sauce

> 2 chicken breast halves, skin and bones removed
> ¼ cup finely chopped onion
> 2 tablespoons butter or margarine
> 1 (10-ounce) package frozen chopped spinach, thawed and drained
> ½ cup shredded Swiss cheese
> ⅛ teaspoon ground nutmeg
> 1⅓ cups sliced mushrooms
> 1½ teaspoons lemon juice
> ½ cup chicken broth
> ½ cup whipping cream
> ¼ cup dry white wine
> Dash of pepper
> Tomato roses and fresh parsley, for garnish

1. Preheat oven to 350°F.

2. Place chicken breasts between two sheets of waxed paper and pound to ¼ inch thick. Set aside.

3. Sauté onion in 1 tablespoon butter in a skillet over medium-high heat.

4. Stir in spinach, cheese, and nutmeg.

5. Divide mixture in half and roll each half into a ball.

6. Place balls in a lightly greased 10 x 6-inch baking dish.

7. Place a chicken breast over each mound.

8. Bake for 20 to 25 minutes, until chicken is done (use fork to see that there is no pink juice).

9. Meanwhile, sauté mushrooms in remaining 1 tablespoon butter in a small saucepan over medium-high heat until liquid evaporates.

10. Add lemon juice, chicken broth, whipping cream, wine, and pepper.

11. Bring to a boil and cook, stirring constantly, for about 7 minutes, or until liquid is reduced by one-third and is slightly thickened.

12. Spoon half of the sauce over each serving of chicken.

13. Garnish each serving with a tomato rose and parsley.

SERVES 2

Note: This recipe can be doubled.

> In many recipes, including this one, finely chopped mushrooms can be substituted for sliced. This is especially useful when serving people who do not care for mushrooms, as their complaint is usually the texture rather than the flavor of mushrooms.

Chicken Scandinavian

> *3 whole chicken breasts, skin and bones removed, halved*
> *6 very thin slices of ham*
> *½ cup flour*
> *½ teaspoon garlic salt*
> *½ teaspoon paprika*
> *4 tablespoons butter or margarine*
> *½ cup chicken broth*
> *½ cup sliced mushrooms*
> *1 cup sour cream*
> *½ cup shredded gjetost cheese*

1. Stack each half chicken breast with a piece of ham, roll it up (chicken side out), and secure with a toothpick.

2. Combine flour, garlic salt, and paprika in a small dish and use to coat the rolled chicken breasts.

3. Melt 2 tablespoons butter in a skillet and brown the chicken quickly on all sides.

4. Add broth to the skillet, cover, and simmer for 25 minutes, or until chicken is tender.

5. Remove chicken from heat and keep warm.

6. Sauté mushrooms in remaining 2 tablespoons butter, until just tender.

7. Blend sour cream with the mushrooms and pan drippings.

8. Stir in cheese and heat slowly until cheese is melted.

9. Pour mushroom-cheese sauce over chicken.

SERVES 4–6

Dilly Chicken and Noodles

1 tablespoon olive oil or vegetable oil
2 whole chicken breasts, skin and bones removed, cut into
  1-inch pieces
1 cup sliced mushrooms
½ cup chopped onion
½ cup chicken broth
2 teaspoons paprika
2 teaspoons chopped fresh dill
¼ teaspoon pepper
1 tablespoon cornstarch
2 tablespoons water
1 (8-ounce) carton plain low-fat yogurt
2 cups hot cooked noodles
1 tablespoon chopped fresh parsley

1. Coat a large frying pan with a cover with cooking spray. Add oil and place over medium heat. Add chicken.

2. Cook chicken 3 to 5 minutes, stirring occasionally, until chicken is lightly browned. Then remove chicken from frying pan.

3. Add mushrooms and onion to frying pan. Sauté over medium-high heat until tender.

4. Return chicken to pan. Add broth, paprika, dill, and pepper.

5. Cover pan and simmer 15 minutes, until chicken is tender.

6. Combine cornstarch and water and stir until smooth.

7. Add cornstarch mixture to frying pan and cook, stirring constantly, until mixture comes to a boil.

8. Cook for 1 minute more, remove from heat, and stir in yogurt.

9. Serve immediately, garnished with parsley, over hot noodles.

SERVES 4

Chicken and Pasta

¼ cup plus 2 tablespoons flour, divided
¾ teaspoon Italian seasoning
¾ teaspoon salt
¼ teaspoon pepper
6 skinless boneless chicken breast halves
4 tablespoons butter or margarine
2 large shallots, chopped
1 garlic clove, minced
8 ounces mushrooms, sliced (about 4 cups)
¼ cup chopped sun-dried tomatoes
1 (14.5-ounce) can chicken broth
¾ cup dry Marsala wine
12 ounces fettuccine pasta
1 tablespoon chopped fresh parsley

1. In a bowl, combine ¼ cup flour, ¼ teaspoon Italian seasoning, ¼ teaspoon salt, and pepper. Set aside.

2. Place each chicken piece between two sheets of plastic wrap and pound each piece to ½ inch thickness.

3. Coat both sides of each piece with flour mixture.

4. Heat a large nonstick skillet over medium-high heat.

5. Melt 1 tablespoon butter.

6. Add 3 pieces of chicken and cook until lightly brown, turning once.

7. Remove from skillet and reserve.

8. Repeat with another 1 tablespoon of butter and remaining chicken.

9. In same skillet melt remaining 2 tablespoons butter.

10. Add shallots, garlic, remaining ½ teaspoon Italian seasoning, and remaining ½ teaspoon salt.

11. Cook until shallots are just softened, about 1 minute.

12. Add mushrooms and tomatoes.

13. Cook, stirring occasionally, until mushrooms are soft and brown, about 3 to 4 minutes.

14. Stir remaining 2 tablespoons flour into broth, and reserve.

15. Add wine to skillet, and cook 1 minute.

16. Stir in broth mixture.

17. Increase heat to high and bring sauce to a boil.

18. Cook, stirring occasionally, until thickened, about 1 minute.

19. Reduce heat to medium-low.

20. Add chicken to the skillet, overlapping pieces slightly if necessary.

21. Cover skillet and cook until chicken is no longer pink in center, 10 to 12 minutes.

22. Meanwhile, cook pasta according to the package directions and drain.

23. Transfer pasta to a platter and top with chicken and mushroom mixture.

24. Sprinkle with parsley.

SERVES 6

Poppy-Seed Chicken

2 pounds skinless boneless chicken breasts
1 (10.75-ounce) can cream of mushroom soup
1 cup sour cream
1 cup finely chopped fresh mushrooms
1 roll Ritz crackers
2 tablespoons poppy seeds
1 stick (8 tablespoons) butter or margarine, melted

1. Preheat oven to 350°F.

2. Boil chicken 8 to 10 minutes. Remove from heat and slice into medium strips.

3. Place chicken in a buttered casserole dish.

4. Mix soup, sour cream, and mushrooms together and pour over chicken.

5. Crush crackers and put on top of casserole.

6. Sprinkle with poppy seeds and drizzle melted butter over.

7. Bake until bubbly.

SERVES 6–8

> To make a complete meal of this recipe, serve it with a tossed green salad or a fruit salad and some crusty bread.

Main Dishes: Seafood

Andy's Clam Spaghetti

1 (8-ounce) package cream cheese
4 tablespoons butter or margarine, softened
3 tablespoons dried basil
3 tablespoons dried parsley
Pepper to taste
¾ tablespoon garlic powder
⅓ cup Parmesan cheese
2 (6.5-ounce) cans chopped clams, drained, juice reserved
⅓ cup sour cream
½ cup sliced mushrooms, sautéed
1 small package spaghetti, cooked
½ cup sliced black olives
½ cup slivered blanched almonds

1. In a double boiler, combine cream cheese with butter and cook over medium-high heat until melted.

2. Add basil, parsley, pepper, and garlic powder.

3. Blend in Parmesan cheese.

4. Stir in clams and ⅔ cup reserved clam juice. Cook until heated through.

5. Add sour cream and sautéed mushrooms. Cook until heated through. (Do not allow sauce to come to a boil.)

6. Serve clam sauce immediately over hot spaghetti, topped with almonds and olives.

SERVES 4–6

English Muffins Topped with Crab and Mushrooms

¾ pound mushrooms, sliced
3 tablespoons butter or margarine
Juice of ½ lemon
¼ cup dry sherry
1 cup sour cream
¾ pound fresh crabmeat or 2 (7.5-ounce) cans crabmeat
3 tablespoons grated Parmesan cheese
4 English muffins
1 tablespoon minced fresh parsley

1. Sauté mushrooms in 1 tablespoon butter and lemon juice in a medium-size skillet over medium-high heat.

2. Add sherry and let cook down until liquid is reduced by one-half.

3. Stir in sour cream and mix until well blended.

4. Add crabmeat and Parmesan cheese. Heat thoroughly.

5. Split English muffins and butter with remaining 2 tablespoons butter. Lightly toast.

6. Arrange English muffins on a serving platter or on individual plates, and spoon on crab mixture.

7. Sprinkle with parsley and serve with salad.

SERVES 4

Tuna Fritters

4 tablespoons butter or margarine
⅓ pound mushrooms, finely sliced
2 (6.5-ounce) cans tuna, drained
½ medium onion, minced
8 rye crisp crackers, crushed
3 eggs
Salt and pepper to taste
Lemon wedges

1. Melt 2 tablespoons butter in a frying pan.

2. Sauté mushrooms in a medium skillet over medium-high heat until tender.

3. Transfer mushrooms to a medium bowl. Add tuna, onion, cracker crumbs, eggs, and salt and pepper. Mix well.

4. Shape tuna into 8 generous patties.

5. Melt remaining 2 tablespoons butter in the frying pan.

6. Cook patties on medium heat until browned on both sides. You may have to do them in batches.

7. Serve patties with lemon wedges.

SERVES 4–6

Halibut Steaks, Italian Style

> ¾ *cup chopped tomato*
> 1½ *cups sliced mushrooms*
> ¼ *cup chopped onion*
> ¼ *cup chopped green pepper*
> 2 *tablespoons minced fresh parsley*
> 1 *garlic clove, minced*
> ½ *teaspoon dried oregano*
> 1 *tablespoon lemon juice*
> 4 *(4-ounce) halibut steaks, with skin*
> ¼ *teaspoon pepper*
> *Lemon slices, halved*

1. Combine tomato, mushrooms, onion, green pepper, parsley, garlic, oregano, and lemon juice in a microwave-safe 12 x 8 x 2-inch baking dish.

2. Stir well and distribute vegetables evenly in the dish.

3. Cover with heavy-duty plastic wrap, folding back a corner of wrap to allow steam to escape.

4. Microwave on high for 4 minutes, turning dish a half turn after 2 minutes.

5. Spoon vegetables to one side of the dish.

6. Arrange fish in dish with thickest portion toward the outside of the dish. Sprinkle with pepper.

7. Spoon vegetables evenly over fish.

8. Cover with heavy-duty plastic wrap, folding back a corner to allow steam to escape.

9. Microwave on high for 4 minutes, turning dish a half turn after 2 minutes.

10. Continue cooking until fish turns opaque.

11. Let stand, covered, for 3 to 5 minutes. (Fish is done if it flakes easily when tested with a fork.)

12. Garnish fish with lemon slices before serving.

SERVES 4

Fish Steaks with Mushroom Caper Sauce

> *6 individual fish steaks (any kind)*
> *4 tablespoons butter or margarine*
> *1½ teaspoons salt*
> *⅛ teaspoon white pepper*
> *1 cup milk*
> *1 pound mushrooms, sliced*
> *3 tablespoons flour*
> *3 tablespoons drained capers*
> *Lemon wedges*

1. Preheat oven to 350°F.

2. Place fish in a greased 12 x 8 x 2-inch baking dish.

3. Dot with 1 tablespoon butter and sprinkle with 1 teaspoon salt and pepper.

4. Cover with heavy-duty aluminum foil and bake until fish flakes easily, approximately 30 minutes.

5. Pour fish stock from pan into a 2-cup glass measuring cup. Add enough milk to the stock to make 2 cups liquid.

6. Cover fish and keep warm.

7. In a large saucepan, melt remaining 3 tablespoons butter.

8. Add mushrooms and sauté for 3 minutes over medium-high heat.

9. Add flour and cook, stirring, for 1 minute more.

10. Blend in fish stock, capers, and remaining ½ teaspoon salt.

11. Boil and stir until sauce is thickened, about 1 minute.

12. Pour sauce over fish steaks and serve with lemon wedges.

SERVES 6

Baked Clams with Mushroom Sauce

½ cup chopped onion
½ cup chopped mushrooms
7 tablespoons butter or margarine
3 cups canned clams
3 tablespoons flour
¼ teaspoon paprika
½ teaspoon salt
⅓ cup chopped fresh parsley
¼ cup fresh dill
1½ cups milk
1 cup buttered bread crumbs

1. Preheat oven to 375°F.

2. Sauté onion and mushrooms in 4 tablespoons butter until onion is translucent.

3. Add clams and cook for 5 minutes. Remove from heat.

4. Melt 3 tablespoons butter in a small saucepan. Add flour, paprika, salt, parsley, and dill. Stir with a wire whisk until well blended to remove any lumps.

5. Slowly add milk while stirring constantly. Bring to boil and boil for 2 minutes.

6. Add to clam mixture.

7. Pour clam mixture into a greased 3-quart casserole dish. Cover with bread crumbs.

8. Bake for 20 to 25 minutes until the bread crumbs are brown.

SERVES 6

Wild Rice and Shrimp Casserole

> *2 cups wild rice*
> *4 tablespoons butter or margarine*
> *1 onion, finely chopped*
> *1 pound medium-size mushrooms*
> *Juice of ½ lemon*
> *2 tablespoons flour*
> *1¼ cups chicken stock*
> *½ cup dry white wine*
> *½ teaspoon salt*
> *¼ teaspoon garlic salt*
> *½ teaspoon dill weed*
> *3 tablespoons Parmesan cheese*
> *1 pound cooked medium shrimp (shelled and deveined)*
> *⅓ pound crab legs, cooked and shelled*
> *1 tablespoon chopped fresh parsley*

1. Preheat oven to 350°F.

2. Wash rice thoroughly under cold water. Put rice in a bowl, add water to cover, and let soak for 1 hour.

3. Cook rice in boiling salted water for 25 minutes, or until almost tender.

4. Melt 2 tablespoons butter in a large frying pan over high heat.

5. Sauté onion until golden.

6. Remove stems from mushrooms (leave caps whole).

7. Add mushroom stems and caps and continue to cook with lemon juice.

8. Cook gently, stirring occasionally, until mushrooms are tender.

9. In another pan, melt remaining 2 tablespoons butter, and then blend in flour and cook over medium heat for 2 to 3 minutes to make a roux.

10. Add chicken stock and wine and cook, stirring constantly, until thickened.

11. Season with salt, garlic salt, dill, and Parmesan cheese.

12. Mix together three-fourths of the sauce, rice, mushrooms, and seafood, reserving a few shrimp and crab legs for garnish.

13. Spoon into a buttered 2-quart casserole.

14. Arrange the remaining shrimp and crab legs on top, and spoon over the remaining sauce.

15. Cover and bake for 20 minutes, or until bubbly.

16. Sprinkle with parsley just before serving.

SERVES 8–10

Note: You can assemble the casserole ahead and refrigerate before cooking. Bake 30 to 35 minutes if cold.

Dried morels are delicious in this dish. When reconstituting, remember to save the liquid by placing it in ice cube trays, freezing, and later placing cubes in a plastic storage bag. These cubes can be used to add wonderful savory flavor to your favorite recipes.

Crab Bake Imperial

6 tablespoons butter or margarine
2 tablespoons flour
½ teaspoon salt
Dash of pepper
1 tablespoon minced fresh parsley
1 tablespoon chopped fresh chives or scallion greens
1 cup milk
1 teaspoon grated lemon peel
2 tablespoons lemon juice
¼ cup chopped mushrooms
2 (7.5-ounce) cans crabmeat
½ cup grated cheddar cheese
½ cup buttered bread crumbs

1. Preheat oven to 350°F.

2. Melt 4 tablespoons butter in a saucepan over medium heat.

3. Blend in flour, salt, pepper, parsley, and chives.

4. Slowly stir in milk and cook for 2 to 3 minutes, or until sauce thickens.

5. Add lemon peel and lemon juice.

6. Sauté mushrooms in remaining 2 tablespoons butter in a medium skillet over medium-high heat until they are soft.

7. Fold mushrooms and crabmeat into sauce.

8. Spoon mixture into individual ramekins or a casserole dish.

9. Sprinkle top with cheese and bread crumbs.

10. Bake for 10 to 15 minutes, or until bubbly and crumbs are brown.

SERVES 4

Seafood Thermidor

1¼ cups sliced mushrooms
4 tablespoons butter or margarine
3 cups cooked seafood (shrimp, lobster, crab, or any combination)
2 (10-ounce) cans condensed cream of mushroom soup
½ teaspoon dry mustard
Dash of cayenne pepper
2 tablespoons grated Parmesan cheese
Paprika, for garnish

1. Preheat oven to 400°F.

2. Sauté mushrooms in butter over medium-high heat until they are soft but not browned.

3. Cut seafood into bite-size pieces. Add to pan with mushrooms.

4. Add soup, mustard, and cayenne to pan and heat thoroughly.

5. Divide mixture among six individual ramekins or turn into a 1½-quart casserole.

6. Sprinkle with cheese and paprika.

7. Bake until hot and bubbly, about 15 minutes.

SERVES 6

Mushroom Seafood Tart

> *Pastry for single-crust pie (your recipe or premade)*
> *1 (7.5-ounce) can minced clams, liquid reserved*
> *½ cup whipping cream*
> *2 tablespoons cornstarch*
> *3 tablespoons dry white wine*
> *⅛ teaspoon nutmeg*
> *4 egg yolks*
> *½ cup grated Parmesan cheese*
> *2 (10-ounce) packages frozen chopped spinach, thawed and*
> *   drained*
> *¼ pound cooked small shrimp*
> *¼ pound mushrooms, sliced*
> *1 garlic clove, minced*
> *2 tablespoons butter or margarine*

1. Preheat oven to 425°F.

2. Prepare pastry shell by placing dough in a 10-inch pie pan or an 11-inch flan pan. Bake for 10 minutes. Remove dough from oven and reduce oven heat to 375°F.

3. Drain liquid from clams into a saucepan.

4. Add whipping cream and bring to a boil.

5. Stir in a paste of cornstarch and wine. Continue cooking over medium high heat, stirring, until thickened.

6. Add nutmeg.

7. Beat egg yolks and stir into the hot sauce, along with 3 table-spoons cheese.

8. Mix in spinach, shrimp, and clams.

9. Sauté mushrooms and garlic in 1 tablespoon of butter in a medium-size skillet over medium-high heat until mushrooms are soft but not browned.

10. Set aside 8 mushroom slices for garnish.

11. Add rest of mushrooms to spinach mixture.

12. Spread filling evenly in baked pastry shell.

13. Top with reserved slices of mushroom and sprinkle with remaining cheese.

14. Melt remaining 1 tablespoon butter and drizzle over top of tart.

15. Bake for 20 to 25 minutes, until set.

SERVES 8

If you're in a mood for experimenting, try substituting another hard cheese, such as Romano, for the Parmesan. You can also make this recipe with your favorite seafood, whether it be scallops or lobster.

Shrimp Risotto

6 tablespoons butter or margarine
1 pound shrimp, peeled and deveined
Juice of 1 lemon
½ small onion, grated
½ cup chopped mushrooms
¼ cup chopped pimientos, preferably Dromedary brand
2 tablespoons flour
3 tablespoons tomato paste
1 cup cream
1 tablespoon salt
Dash of pepper
6 drops Worcestershire sauce
4 cups cooked rice
½ cup chopped black olives
Fresh parsley, for garnish

1. Melt 4 tablespoons butter in a heavy skillet.

2. Cut shrimp in half lengthwise, and sprinkle lemon juice over shrimp.

3. Add shrimp to skillet and cook, stirring, for 3 minutes.

4. Remove shrimp from heat and keep warm.

5. Melt remaining 2 tablespoons butter in skillet.

6. Add onion and mushrooms, and cook, stirring, over medium heat for 3 minutes. Add pimientos.

7. Remove skillet from heat. Stir in flour and tomato paste, then add cream, salt, pepper, and Worcestershire sauce.

8. Return skillet to heat and stir mixture until it thickens.

9. Add shrimp and pour over rice. Garnish with olives and parsley.

SERVES 6–8

Scallops St-Jacques

1 pound scallops
1 cup dry white wine
A few sprigs fresh parsley
Celery tops
Onion slices
Salt and pepper to taste
1 stick (8 tablespoons) butter or margarine
2 tablespoons flour
1 cup milk
6 tablespoons grated Parmesan cheese, divided
6 tablespoons Swiss cheese, divided
¼ pound mushrooms, sliced

1. Preheat oven to 450°F.

2. In a small pan, cover scallops with wine. Add parsley, celery tops, onion slices, and salt and pepper. Simmer 5 minutes.

3. Divide scallops among 4 individual ramekins or scallop shells. Reserve liquid.

4. For Mornay sauce, melt butter in a small saucepan, then add flour, whisking out all lumps. Slowly add milk, stirring constantly, and bring to a boil. Add 2 tablespoons Parmesan and 2 tablespoons Swiss cheese. Warm over low heat, stirring, until blended.

5. Boil scallop liquid to reduce by half and strain. Add scallop liquid and mushrooms to Mornay sauce.

6. Spoon sauce over scallops in ramekins.

7. Sprinkle scallops with remaining 4 tablespoons Parmesan and 4 tablespoons Swiss cheese. Bake in hot oven until topping melts and browns.

SERVES 4

Lobster Newburg for Two

2 frozen rock lobster tails (about 8 ounces each), thawed
1 tablespoon butter or margarine
1½ cups sliced mushrooms
¼ cup dry sherry
½ cup cream
½ cup frozen baby peas, cooked
¼ teaspoon salt
Pinch of cayenne pepper
2 slices of toast, cut in half
Paprika, for garnish

1. In covered 4-quart saucepan, heat 1½ inches of water to boiling.

2. Add lobster tails, cover, and return to a boil.

3. Reduce heat to medium and cook for 7 minutes, or until lobster meat is opaque throughout.

4. Meanwhile, in a nonstick 12-inch skillet, melt butter over medium-high heat.

5. Add mushrooms and cook 5 minutes, or until brown.

6. Transfer mushrooms to a bowl.

7. Add sherry to the skillet and boil 1 minute.

8. Add cream and cook 3 minutes, or until sauce thickens slightly.

9. Add peas, salt, cayenne, and mushrooms.

10. Remove from heat.

11. Cut away and discard thin underside shell and small flippers on each lobster tail. Remove meat in one piece.

12. Cut lobster meat crosswise into ¼-inch-thick slices.

13. Add lobster to sauce and heat through.

14. Place toast on plates and cover with lobster mixture.

15. Sprinkle with paprika.

Serves 2

Any available mushrooms may be used in this recipe, but morels, shiitake, chanterelles, oyster mushrooms, and porcini are particularly marvelous.

Main Dishes: Eggs and Cheese

Artichoke and Cheese Strata

½ *cup sliced mushrooms*
½ *cup chopped scallions*
1 *tablespoon butter or margarine*
3 *slices white bread, cubed*
¾ *cup shredded sharp cheddar cheese*
1 *(14-ounce) can artichoke hearts, drained and quartered*
1 *(4-ounce) jar pimientos, preferably Dromedary brand*
4 *eggs, beaten*
1½ *cups milk*
½ *teaspoon dry mustard*
Salt and pepper to taste

1. Sauté mushrooms and scallions in butter in a small skillet over medium-high heat until tender. Set aside.

2. Layer half of bread cubes, mushroom mixture, cheese, artichokes, and pimientos in a lightly greased 9-inch quiche dish.

3. Repeat layers.

4. Combine eggs, milk, mustard, and salt and pepper; mix well.

5. Pour egg mixture over vegetables in baking dish.

6. Cover and chill strata 3 hours.

7. Remove strata from refrigerator and let stand 30 minutes. Preheat oven to 350°F.

8. Bake strata, uncovered, for 50 to 55 minutes, or until set.

9. Let stand 10 minutes before serving.

SERVES 6

Chile Cheese Bake

½ pound cheddar cheese
½ pound Monterey Jack cheese
1 (7-ounce) can whole green chiles
¼ pound mushrooms, sliced
1 tablespoon butter or margarine
8 eggs

1. Preheat oven to 350°F.

2. Grate cheeses and mix together in a bowl.

3. Put half of the cheese in a buttered 12 x 7½ x 2-inch baking pan.

4. Split the chiles in half and lay them on top of the cheese.

5. Sauté mushrooms in butter in a small skillet over medium-high heat until soft. Spread mushrooms over chiles.

6. Sprinkle remainder of cheese over the top of the mushrooms.

7. Blend eggs in a blender for 15 seconds.

8. Pour eggs over cheese.

9. Bake for 30 minutes, or until set.

10. Cut into squares to serve.

SERVES 6–8

Note: This recipe needs no extra seasonings; the chile and cheese are sufficient.

Frittata con Fungi

> *6–8 fresh morels*
> *3 tablespoons olive oil or vegetable oil*
> *⅓ cup chopped onion*
> *1–2 garlic cloves, finely chopped*
> *1 tablespoon butter or margarine*
> *¼ medium red bell pepper, chopped*
> *4 whole eggs*
> *¼ cup milk*
> *¼ cup grated Parmesan cheese*
> *Salt and pepper to taste*

1. Cut mushrooms into small to medium pieces.

2. Heat 2 tablespoons oil in a medium-size frying pan over medium-high heat.

3. Sauté half of the onion and all the garlic, making sure the garlic does not burn, until onion is translucent.

4. Add morels and cook over medium heat until they give up their water.

5. Turn the heat to high and cook until the water has evaporated and mushrooms pop. Remove from heat and set aside.

8. In a 10-inch nonstick ovensafe frying pan, melt butter along with remaining 1 tablespoon oil. Heat until butter foams.

9. Add bell pepper and remaining onion.

10. Sauté until onion is translucent.

11. Combine eggs, milk, cheese, mushrooms, and salt and pepper in a bowl and beat.

12. Add this mixture to the frying pan.

13. Cook over medium-low heat until eggs have set and thickened. Preheat the broiler.

14. When only the surface of the eggs is runny, place pan in oven under the broiler.

15. Remove from broiler when top of the frittata is set and top has begun to brown.

16. Loosen the frittata with a spatula and slide onto a platter. Cut into pie-shape serving wedges.

SERVES 4–5

Note: Dried morels can be substituted if steeped in warm water for 20 to 30 minutes and then cooked as above. Remember to save the liquid from rehydrating the mushrooms. Strain the liquid and freeze it in ice cube trays to use later in sauces.

For a lower-cholesterol variation, make an egg-white fritatta. Simply substitute 2–3 egg whites for 2 of the whole eggs and prepare as described.

Eggs au Gratin

4 hard-boiled eggs
4 tablespoons butter or margarine
¼ cup sliced mushrooms
2 tablespoons flour
1 cup milk
¼ teaspoon salt
¼ cup grated mild American cheese
2 tablespoons toasted bread crumbs

1. Preheat oven to 350°F.

2. Cut eggs in half lengthwise and place in a small buttered baking dish.

3. Melt 2 tablespoons butter in a saucepan.

4. Sauté mushrooms in a small skillet over medium-high heat until soft. Set aside.

5. Melt remaining 2 tablespoons butter in another saucepan over medium-high heat.

6. Stir in flour and cook until thick and bubbly.

7. Gradually stir in milk, and cook until smooth and thick. Add salt.

8. Add mushrooms to cream sauce and pour over eggs. Top with cheese and sprinkle bread crumbs over all.

9. Bake 15 minutes, or until cheese is melted.

SERVES 4

Maxine's Mushroom Casserole

1 pound mushrooms, sliced
1 cup chopped celery
½ cup chopped green pepper
½ cup chopped onion
4 tablespoons butter or margarine
1 tablespoon dried dill or parsley
½ teaspoon salt
Dash of pepper
3 eggs, beaten
2 cups milk
3 French rolls or 6 slices of bread, cubed
½ cup grated Parmesan cheese

1. Preheat oven to 350°F.

2. Sauté mushrooms, celery, green pepper, and onion in butter in a nonstick pan over medium-high heat until soft and onion is translucent.

3. Add dill, salt, pepper, eggs, milk, and bread.

4. Pour mixture into a 2-quart casserole and top with cheese.

5. Bake 50 to 60 minutes, or until bubbly and the cheese is browned.

SERVES 4–5

Vegetable Soufflé

5 eggs
2 cups milk
2 cups Chablis wine
2 cups cubed whole wheat bread
1 head broccoli, chopped
2 teaspoons salt
1 teaspoon onion powder
½ teaspoon garlic powder
½ teaspoon dried sweet basil
2 cups grated Colby cheese
2 stalks celery, sliced
½ pound mushrooms, sliced

1. Preheat oven to 375°F.

2. To make custard sauce, mix eggs, milk, and wine. Beat with a wire whisk and set aside.

3. Oil a 3-quart baking dish.

4. Layer bread, broccoli, salt, onion powder, garlic powder, and basil in baking dish.

5. Next, add a thin layer of cheese, celery, mushrooms, and the rest of the cheese. Spread evenly.

6. Pour on custard sauce.

7. Bake for 1½ hours, or until custard is set. Serve as a casserole.

SERVES 4

No-Sauce Mushroom Macaroni and Cheese

½ pound mushrooms, sliced
1 small onion, finely chopped
1 stick (8 tablespoons) butter or margarine
1 (8-ounce) box of macaroni
2 teaspoons salt
2 cups milk
3 eggs
8 ounces grated sharp cheese
Paprika, for garnish

1. Preheat oven to 350°F.

2. Sauté mushrooms and onion in 2 tablespoons butter in a medium-size skillet over medium-high heat until mushrooms are soft and onion is translucent. Set aside.

3. Cook macaroni according to instructions on the box.

4. Drain but do not rinse.

5. Place macaroni in a greased 2-quart casserole.

6. Mix salt, milk, and eggs with an eggbeater. Set aside.

7. Sprinkle most of the cheese into the macaroni.

8. Cut the remaining 6 tablespoons butter into small pieces and add to the macaroni. Mix with a fork.

9. Pour milk and egg mixture over macaroni.

10. Sprinkle rest of cheese over top and sprinkle lightly with paprika.

11. Bake until firm and brown on top.

SERVES 8–10

Low Fat Microwave Spinach-Mushroom Quiche

1 (10-ounce) package frozen chopped spinach, thawed
1 cup egg substitute
½ cup sliced mushrooms
½ cup chopped onion
Dash of salt and pepper
Dash of ground nutmeg
4 teaspoons grated Parmesan cheese

1. Combine spinach, egg substitute, mushrooms, onion, salt and pepper, and nutmeg.

2. Spray two 2-cup microwave bowls with cooking spray. Fill each with half of the spinach mixture.

3. Cover each bowl with plastic wrap, folding back one corner to allow steam to escape.

4. Microwave on 50-percent power for 6 minutes.

5. Rotate dishes one half turn halfway through cooking.

6. Sprinkle each portion with 2 teaspoons Parmesan cheese before serving.

SERVES 2

Mushroom Medley

1 cup shredded Gruyère cheese
1 cup shredded cheddar cheese
½ cup sour cream
½ cup cottage cheese
1 medium onion, finely chopped
1 teaspoon dried thyme
4 large potatoes, thinly sliced
½ pound mushrooms, sliced
2 tablespoons flour
Salt and pepper to taste
¼ cup wheat germ
3 tablespoons butter or margarine

1. Preheat oven to 350°F.

2. Combine cheeses, sour cream, cottage cheese, onion, and thyme in a medium bowl.

3. Arrange one-third of the potatoes in a buttered shallow 2-quart baking dish.

4. Top with half of the cheese mixture.

5. Toss mushrooms with flour and arrange half of them over cheese.

6. Season with salt and pepper.

7. Repeat layers, ending with potatoes.

8. Sprinkle with wheat germ and dot with butter.

9. Bake for 1½ hours or until potatoes are tender.

10. Let stand 10 minutes before serving.

SERVES 4

Main Dishes: Vegetable

Cauliflower and Mushroom Casserole

1 medium head cauliflower, approximately 2½ pounds, cut
 into florets
1½ pounds mushrooms, halved
1 stick (8 tablespoons) butter or margarine
6 tablespoons flour
1 teaspoon salt
2½ cups milk, scalded
1⅓ cups grated sharp cheese
⅓ cup Parmesan cheese
½ cup sherry
Paprika, for garnish
½ cup chopped fresh parsley

1. Preheat oven to 350°F.

2. Cook cauliflower in boiling water in a large saucepan until
   tender.

3. Sauté mushrooms in 2 tablespoons butter in a medium-size
   skillet over medium-high heat until mushrooms are tender but
   not crisp.

4. Combine mushrooms and cauliflower in a 1½-quart casserole
   dish.

5. For the cheese sauce, melt 6 tablespoons butter in a heavy
   saucepan over low heat.

6. Stir in flour and salt and cook for at least 1 minute.

7. Stir in scalded milk and cook over medium heat, stirring
   constantly, until thickened and smooth.

8. Remove from heat and stir in cheeses and sherry.

9. Pour cheese sauce over casserole and stir gently.

10. Sprinkle with paprika.

11. Cook casserole for 30 minutes or until bubbly. Sprinkle with parsley.

SERVES 6–8

For something a little different, try cooking the mushrooms with bouillon or broth instead of sautéing them in fat. This is a great way to reduce the calories and to use some of those mushroom-broth cubes you've got in the freezer.

Mushroom Lasagna

> 2 strips bacon, chopped
> 2 scallions, chopped
> 2 sticks (16 tablespoons) butter or margarine
> 1 teaspoon thyme
> 2 pounds mushrooms, sliced
> 3 cups milk
> 1 bay leaf
> 1 cup chicken broth
> ⅔ cup flour
> 1 cup shredded Swiss cheese
> ⅓ cup grated Parmesan cheese
> ⅛ teaspoon nutmeg
> 1 pound lasagna noodles

1. Preheat oven to 350°F.

2. Cook bacon in a large saucepan over medium-high heat until crisp. Transfer bacon to a medium-size bowl.

3. Add scallions to saucepan and sauté over medium-high heat until translucent.

4. Remove scallions and add to bowl with bacon.

5. Melt 4 tablespoons butter in bacon fat in the saucepan.

6. Add thyme and half the mushrooms.

7. Sauté over medium-high heat until soft and lightly browned and then add to bacon mixture.

8. Sauté remaining mushrooms in another 4 tablespoons butter and add to the bacon mixture.

9. For the sauce, scald milk with bay leaf and cool slightly.

10. Make a roux by melting remaining 8 tablespoons butter in a large frying pan. Add flour and cook over medium-high heat, stirring constantly, until brown and bubbly.

11. Add milk and chicken broth while stirring, and cook over medium-high heat until thickened.

12. Add cheeses and nutmeg.

13. Stir until smooth.

14. Boil 1 pound lasagna noodles until slightly undercooked.

15. Butter a 9 x 13-inch baking dish. Layer 1 cup sauce, one-third of the noodles, and half the mushroom mixture. Repeat layers, ending with lasagna noodles and sauce.

16. Bake covered for 45 minutes, or until bubbly. Cool slightly and allow to set before serving.

SERVES 6–8

Mushroom Loaf

> 2 pounds mushrooms, chopped (including stems; reserve several
>   caps for garnish)
> 1 large onion, thinly sliced
> 10 tablespoons butter or margarine
> ½ cup dry bread crumbs
> ½ teaspoon salt
> Dash of pepper
> 2 eggs, lightly beaten

1. Preheat oven to 350°F.

2. Sauté mushrooms and onion in 2 tablespoons butter in a large skillet over medium-high heat until golden brown.

3. Mix mushrooms, onion, bread crumbs, salt, and pepper. Melt remaining 8 tablespoons butter and stir in.

4. Stir in eggs.

5. Press entire mixture into a well-greased loaf pan.

6. Arrange mushroom caps on top and press slightly.

7. Bake for 1 hour, or until loaf shrinks away from the edges slightly.

8. Let stand for several minutes.

9. Slice loaf and serve with mushroom gravy.

SERVES 6–8

Portobello Mushroom Fries

> *4 large portobello mushroom caps*
> *¼ cup olive oil or vegetable oil, plus more for drizzling*
> *Salt and pepper to taste or steak seasonings of choice*
> *2 eggs, beaten*
> *¼ cup chopped fresh cilantro*
> *1 cup Italian bread crumbs*
> *½ cup shredded or grated Parmesan cheese*

1. Preheat a grill pan over medium-high to high heat.

2. Scrape gills from the portobello caps with a spoon.

3. Brush caps gently with a damp cloth.

4. Drizzle caps with oil to keep them from sticking to the grill.

5. Season with salt and pepper or steak seasoning.

6. Grill mushrooms 3 or 4 minutes on each side, covered by a tinfoil tent.

7. Remove from heat and cool 5 minutes.

8. Slice mushrooms into ½-inch strips.

9. Dip mushrooms in egg and coat with a mixture of cilantro, bread crumbs, and cheese.

10. Heat remaining ¼ cup oil over medium heat in a nonstick skillet.

11. Fry mushrooms until brown, about 2 or 3 minutes on each side.

SERVES 4

Eggplant and Mushroom Casserole

2½ cups diced eggplant
⅔ cup olive oil or vegetable oil
¾ cup thinly sliced onion
2 garlic cloves, sliced
1 cup sliced mushrooms
½ cup whole pitted black olives
4 green peppers, julienned
3 cups sliced zucchini (½-inch slices)
2 cups skinned, seeded, and quartered tomatoes
½ teaspoon dried oregano or 2 teaspoons chopped fresh basil
Salt and pepper to taste
Sour cream

1. Salt eggplant to get rid of excess moisture.

2. Place cubes on a rack and let drain or place cubes on a plate and weight them so moisture will be squeezed out.

3. Heat olive oil in a deep skillet.

4. Sauté onion and garlic over medium-high heat until onion is translucent.

5. Add mushrooms, olives, green peppers, zucchini, tomatoes, eggplant, and oregano or basil.

6. Simmer, covered, over very low heat for about 45 minutes.

7. Uncover and continue to cook for 15 minutes to reduce the amount of liquid.

8. Salt and pepper to taste.

9. Serve casserole hot or cold with a dollop of sour cream.

SERVES 6–8

Mushroom-Spinach Casserole

1 pound whole mushrooms
1 (8-ounce) can water chestnuts, sliced and drained
1 (14-ounce) can artichoke hearts, quartered
2 (8-ounce) packages of cream cheese
1 stick (8 tablespoons) butter or margarine
4 (10-ounce) packages frozen chopped spinach, cooked and well
   drained
Juice of 1 lemon
Salt and pepper to taste
Seasoned bread crumbs

1. Preheat oven to 350°F.

2. Butter a 3-quart casserole dish.

3. Cover bottom of casserole with mushrooms, water chestnuts, and artichoke hearts.

4. Melt together cream cheese and butter in a saucepan over medium-high heat.

5. Stir in spinach, lemon juice, and salt and pepper.

6. Pour spinach mixture over vegetables in casserole dish. Top with seasoned bread crumbs.

7. Bake for 25 to 30 minutes, or until casserole is bubbly and bread crumbs are browned.

SERVES 20

Note: This recipe can be halved.

Mushroom-Stuffed Manicotti

10 manicotti shells
1 (10-ounce) package frozen chopped spinach
6 ounces mushrooms
1½ cups ricotta cheese
2 eggs, slightly beaten
1 small onion, chopped
2 garlic cloves, minced
½ teaspoon salt
¼ teaspoon pepper
Dash of Tabasco sauce
½ cup Parmesan cheese
1 (6-ounce) can tomato paste
1 cup water
1 teaspoon Italian herb seasoning

1. Preheat oven to 375°F.

2. Cook manicotti shells according to package directions.

3. Thaw spinach and squeeze out liquid.

4. Slice mushrooms into ¼-inch slices.

5. Mix together mushrooms, spinach, ricotta, eggs, onion, garlic, salt, pepper, Tabasco sauce, and two-thirds of Parmesan cheese.

6. Fill each shell with mixture and place in a shallow baking dish.

7. In a bowl, combine tomato paste, water, and seasoning. Pour over shells.

8. Sprinkle with remaining Parmesan cheese.

9. Bake for 35 minutes, or until manicotti is bubbly and cheese has browned.

SERVES 4–5

Miscellaneous Delights

Bob's Microwave Morels

Morels
Butter or margarine
Salt and pepper to taste
Dill weed

1. Place fresh morels in a bowl.

2. Add butter or margarine, salt and pepper, and dill.

3. Heat on high for approximately 30 seconds (longer if you have a lot of morels).

4. Serve with toothpicks.

SERVING SIZE DEPENDS ON THE NUMBER OF MORELS

Herbed Mushroom Pâté

  3 cups chopped onion
  4 tablespoons butter or margarine
  1 pound chopped Coprinus comatus *("shaggy manes"; other*
    mushrooms can be used, as well)
  ½ teaspoon salt
  1 teaspoon dry mustard
  ½ teaspoon dill weed
  Pepper to taste
  3 tablespoons dry white wine
  2 cups cottage cheese
  1 (8-ounce) package cream cheese, softened
  Paprika, for garnish
  Fresh parsley, for garnish
  Toast and/or crackers

1. Preheat oven to 400°F. Butter two 4 x 8-inch loaf pans and line with buttered waxed paper.

2. Sauté onion in butter in a medium-size skillet over medium-high heat until soft.

3. Add mushrooms, salt, mustard, dill, and pepper.

4. Stir and cook uncovered for 5 minutes.

5. Add wine and cook for 5 minutes more.

6. Set aside.

7. In a blender, puree cottage cheese until smooth and transfer to a large bowl.

8. Cream the cream cheese until soft enough to blend.

9. Combine the two cheese mixtures.

10. Puree the mushroom mixture until almost smooth.

11. Add it to the cheese mixture, stirring well.

12. Spoon mixture into prepared loaf pans.

13. Bake for 1¼ hours.

14. Cool in pan and then remove and peel off waxed paper.

15. Chill covered for at least four hours before serving.

16. Sprinkle loaves with paprika and chopped parsley.

17. Serve with toast or crackers.

YIELDS 2 LOAVES

Hints for purchasing and storing mushrooms: Make sure the mushrooms you purchase are firm, dry, and free from too much discoloration. Always buy mushrooms displayed in open baskets and not in plastic. Never buy or use mushrooms that are slick or slimy. Put your mushrooms in brown paper bags before putting them in the refrigerator; fold the bag over and the mushrooms will keep longer without getting slimy.

Chanterelle Biscuits

2 cups flour
5 teaspoons baking powder
½ teaspoon salt
4 tablespoons Crisco shortening
¼ cup chopped onion or chives
½ cup grated Parmesan cheese
½ cup finely chopped cooked chanterelles
¼ cup milk
4 tablespoons butter, melted

1. Preheat oven to 400°F.

2. Mix flour, baking powder, and salt. Cut in shortening.

3. Add onion, cheese, and mushrooms. Knead lightly.

4. Add milk and blend.

5. Form in a ball and knead lightly.

6. Press dough out to a thickness of ¼ to ½ inch.

7. Cut into rounds with a 3-inch biscuit cutter.

8. Brush both sides of biscuits with melted butter.

9. Bake for 12 to 15 minutes, or until golden brown.

YIELDS 1 DOZEN BISCUITS

Mole Sauce

1 cup mushrooms, sliced
8 garlic cloves, chopped
2 tablespoons olive oil or vegetable oil
½ cup dry red wine
1 (10.5-ounce) can condensed beef broth
⅓ cup soy sauce
1 tablespoon semisweet chocolate morsels

1. Sauté mushrooms and garlic in hot oil in a medium-size saucepan over high heat until crisp-tender. Drain.

2. Stir in red wine, beef broth, soy sauce, and chocolate.

3. Bring mixture to a boil.

4. Reduce heat and simmer, stirring occasionally, for 30 minutes.

5. Serve over your favorite Mexican dishes.

YIELDS ⅔ CUP

Pickled Catathelasma

Catathelasma *mushrooms ("potato mushrooms")*
2 cups red wine vinegar
½ cup olive oil or vegetable oil
6 garlic cloves, thinly sliced
1 teaspoon salt
½ teaspoon crushed peppercorns
¼ teaspoon thyme
4 tablespoons chopped fresh parsley
1 tablespoon oregano

1. Cut mushrooms into ¼-inch slices.

2. Combine remaining ingredients to make pickling mix. Bring pickling mix to a boil.

3. Add mushrooms and simmer about 15 minutes.

4. Pack mushrooms and pickling mix in sterile jars and follow instructions for pressure canning (see your canner's instructions for times).

5. Serve as a condiment with dinners or lunches.

MAKES 2–3 JARS OF PICKLES, DEPENDING ON THE SIZE AND NUMBER OF MUSHROOMS

Puffball Chips

2 *pounds young puffballs, pure white inside, cleaned and peeled*
1 *tablespoon salt*
1 *tablespoon pepper*
½ *teaspoon sweet Hungarian paprika*
12 *tablespoons butter or margarine, melted*

1. Slice puffballs very thin.

2. Mix salt, pepper, and paprika and use to dust puffball slices.

3. Fry in melted butter in a large skillet over high heat until golden brown and crispy.

4. Drain chips and dry on paper towels.

5. Store cooled chips in tightly sealed glass jars. Serve as snacks in the place of potato chips.

SERVES 16

Metric Conversion Tables
METRIC U.S. APPROXIMATE EQUIVALENTS

Liquid Ingredients

METRIC	U.S. MEASURES	METRIC	U.S. MEASURES
1.23 ML	¼ TSP.	29.57 ML	2 TBSP.
2.36 ML	½ TSP.	44.36 ML	3 TBSP.
3.70 ML	¾ TSP.	59.15 ML	¼ CUP
4.93 ML	1 TSP.	118.30 ML	½ CUP
6.16 ML	1¼ TSP.	236.59 ML	1 CUP
7.39 ML	1½ TSP.	473.18 ML	2 CUPS OR 1 PT
8.63 ML	1¾ TSP.	709.77 ML	3 CUPS
9.86 ML	2 TSP.	946.36 ML	4 CUPS OR 1 QT
14.79 ML	1 TBSP.	3.79 L	4 QTS. OR 1 GA

Dry Ingredients

METRIC	U.S. MEASURES	METRIC	U.S. MEASURES
2 (1.8) G	¹⁄₁₆ OZ.	80 G	2⅘ OZ.
3½ (3.5) G	⅛ OZ.	85 (84.9) G	3 OZ.
7 (7.1) G	¼ OZ.	100 G	3½ OZ.
15 (14.2) G	½ OZ.	115 (113.2) G	4 OZ.
21 (21.3) G	¾ OZ.	125 G	4½ OZ.
25 G	⅞ OZ.	150 G	5¼ OZ.
30 (28.3) G	1 OZ.	250 G	8⅞ OZ.
50 G	1¾ OZ.	454 G 1 LB.	16 OZ.
60 (56.6) G	2 OZ.	500 G 1 LIVRE	17⅗ OZ.

GLOSSARY

Agaric: mushroom with gills where spores are borne

Annular ring: a distinct ring on the stalk

Attached gills: gills that are borne from the underside of the cap and are attached directly to the stalk

Boletinoid: radially arranged and elongated pores, as in *Suillus*

Bulb: a swollen base of the stalk

Buttons: immature mushrooms

Cespitose: several clusters of fruiting bodies growing next to one another but not fused at the base

Close: describes the spacing of gills; halfway between crowded and subdistant

Conks: perennial, woody fruiting bodies; usually growing on trees, etc.

Conifer: a cone-bearing tree, such as a pine or spruce

Crowded: very close spacing of the gills

Decurrent: gills extending the stalk

Depressed: having the disc lower than the margin of the cap or tubes sunken around the stalk

Disc: the central portion of the surface of the cap

Distant: very wide spacing of the gills

Duff: cast-off needles and plant parts on the forest floor

Eccentric: attached off-center, referring to the stipe placement on the substrate

Fairy ring: a ring of mushrooms growing from the threads of fungus tissue found in a grassy area. Each year they use up the nutrients in the grass and grow into larger circles.

Fibrillose: having fibrils

Foray: a field trip to collect mushrooms

Free gills: gills that do not attach to the stalk; for example, those of *Amanita*

Fruiting body: the entire portion of a fungus developed for production of spores

Genus: a group of closely related similar species; for example, *Amanita*

Glabrous: smooth; bald; lacking scales, fibrils, etc.

Globose: round

Glutinous: sticky, gluelike, covered with pectinous material

Hardwoods: trees with broad leaves; for example, birch, beech, oak, aspen, maple

Humus: partially decomposed plant material

Hyphae: microscopic, threadlike filaments

Latex: a juice that can be milky or watery, white or colored; see *Lactarius*

Locules: small round cells that contain the spores in a puffball or earth ball

Mycelium: collective name for the filamentous threads of the vegetative fungus plant

Mycorrhizal: a fungus whose mycelium have a symbiotic relationship with the tiny, short roots of green plants

Parasite: a fungus that attacks living tissue of a plant or animal and kills it. A true parasite kills the substrate and saprophyte decays the tissue.

Partial veil: a covering that extends from the unopened margin of the mushroom cap to the stalk

Plane: having a flat surface

Recurved: a term used by mycologists to indicate incurved

Rhizomorph: a cord or strand composed of mycelium, which penetrates the substrate

Spore print: a deposit of spores left on paper when the cap is placed on it; used to detect the spore color

Sterile base: the interior of a puffball that does not produce spores

Subdistant: describes spacing of the gills; between close and distant

Substrate: whatever the mushroom is growing on, such as wood, dirt, tree bark, nuts, etc.

Tomentose: densely matted or wooly

Tubes: tiny hollow cylinders in which the spores of boletes or polypores are produced

Umbo: a knob or abruptly raised area in the center of a mushroom cap

Universal veil: a tissue surrounding the mushroom button

Viscid: sticky to the touch

Volva: the remains of the universal veil, located at or surrounding the base of the stalk or as patches on the cap of a fungus

BIBLIOGRAPHY

Bessette, A. E., O. K. Miller, A. R. Bessette, and H.H. Miller. 1995. *Mushrooms of North America in Color: A Field Guide Companion to Seldom-Illustrated Fungi.* Syracuse University Press: Syracuse, NY. 172p.

Bessette, A. E., W. C. Roody, and A. R. Bessette. 2000. *North American Boletes.* Syracuse University Press: Syracuse, NY. 396p.

Binion, D. E., S. L. Stephenson, W. C. Roody, H. H. Burdsall Jr., O. K. Miller Jr., and L. N. Vasilyeva. 2008. *Macrofungi Associated with Oaks of Eastern North America.* West Virginia University Press: Morgantown. 467p.

Evenson, V. S. 1997. *Mushrooms of Colorado and the Southern Rocky Mountains.* Westcliffe Publishers: Boulder, CO. 207p.

Hall, I. R., S. L. Stephenson, P. K. Buchanan, W. Yun, and A. L. J. Cole. 2003. *Edible and Poisonous Mushrooms of the World.* Timber Press, Inc.: Christchurch, New Zealand. 371p.

Huffman, D. M., L. H. Tiffany, G. Knaphus, and R. A. Healy. 2008. *Mushrooms and Other Fungi of the Midcontinental United States.* University of Iowa Press: Iowa City, IA. 370p.

Kimbrough, J. 2000. *Common Florida Mushrooms.* University of Florida Extension: Gainesville, FL. 342p.

Lincoff, G., and D. H. Mitchel. 1977. *Toxic and Hallucinogenic Mushroom Poisoning.* Van Nostrand Reinhold Co.: New York. 267p.

Metzler, S., V. T. Metzler, and O. K. Miller Jr. 1992. *Mushrooms of Texas.* University of Texas Press: Austin. 350p.

Miller, H. H. 1993. *Hope's Mushroom Cookbook.* Mad River Press: Eureka, CA. 220p.

Miller, O. K., Jr. 1977. *Mushrooms of North America.* E.P. Dutton, Inc.: New York. 350p.

Miller, O. K., Jr., and H. H. Miller. 1980. *Mushrooms in Color: How to Know Them, Where to Find Them, What to Avoid.* E. P. Dutton, Inc.: New York. 286p.

Bibliography

Miller, O. K., Jr., and H. H. Miller. 1988. *Gasteromycetes: Morphological and Developmental Features with Keys to the Orders, Families, and Genera.* Mad River Press: Eureka, CA. 157p.

Miller, O. K., Jr., and H. H. Miller. 2006. *North American Mushrooms: A Field Guide to Edible and Inedible Fungi.* Falcon Field Guide: Guilford, CT. 583p.

Pomerleau, R. 1980. *Flora Des Champignons au Québec.* Les Éditions la Presse: Ottawa, Canada. 623p.

Roody, W. C. 2003. *Mushrooms of West Virginia and the Central Appalachians.* University Press of Kentucky: Lexington. 520p.

Spoerke, D. G., and R. H. Rumack. 1994. *Handbook of Mushroom Poisoning, Diagnosis, and Treatment.* CRC Press: West Palm Beach, FL. 456p.

Trudell, S., and J. Ammirati. 2009. *Mushrooms of the Pacific Northwest.* Timber Press, Inc.: Portland, OR. 349p.

RECIPE LIST

INDEX

Index

Index

No-Sauce Mushrooms,
   Macaroni, and Cheese, 187
Vegetable Soufflé, 186
Eggs au Gratin, 184
emergency rooms, xiv–xv
English Muffins Topped with
   Crab and Mushrooms, 164
enoki agaric mushroom, 49
enokitake agaric mushroom, 49
eucalyptus, xiv

F

Finnish Mushroom Salad, 101
Fish Steaks with Mushroom
   Caper Sauce, 168
Flammulina velutipes (winter
   mushroom, velvet foot, and
   enoki agarics), 49
French Onion Soup with
   Mushrooms, 99
Frittata con Fungi, 182–83

G

gemmed puffball mushroom, 16
German Potato Salad, 102
giant polypore mushroom, 31
giant puffball mushroom, 12
Ginger Chicken and
   Mushrooms, 151
golden chanterelle
   mushroom, 40
Gomphus clavatus (pig's
   ear), 44
Greek Chicken Breasts with
   Mushrooms, 149
Green Bean and Mushroom
   Salad, 116
green death cap agaric
   mushroom, 58

green-spored lepiota agaric
   mushroom, 59
Grifola frondosa (hen of the
   woods), 28, 31
Gyromitra ambigua, 9
Gyromitra esculenta (common
   false morel), 9
Gyromitra gigas, 10
Gyromitra montana (snow morel),
   8, 10

H

*H. erinaceus ssp. erinaceo-
   abietus,* 37
half-free morel mushroom, 7
Halibut Steaks, Italian Style,
   166–67
ham
   Ham and Cheese Strata,
      134–35
   Ham and Mushroom Pizza, 138
   Ham and Shrimp Curry,
      132–33
Ham and Cheese Strata, 134–35
Ham and Mushroom Pizza, 138
Ham and Shrimp Curry, 132–33
hen of the woods polypore
   mushroom, 28
Herbed Mushroom Pâté,
   200–201
Herbes de Provence, 135
Hericium coralloides (Coralloid
   hericium), 38
Hericium erinaceus (lion's
   mane), 37
hollow stem suillus bolete
   mushroom, 23
horn of plenty chanterelle
   mushroom, 42
Hot Chicken Cobbler, 152

Index

Index

ABOUT THE AUTHOR

Hope H. Miller has coauthored three mushroom books with her late husband, Orson K. Miller Jr.: *North American Mushrooms* (FalconGuides); *Mushrooms in Color: How to Know Them, Where to Find Them, What to Avoid*; and *Gasteromycetes*. She coauthored *Mushrooms of North America in Color: A Field Guide Companion to Seldom Illustrated Fungi* with Alan E. Bessette, Orson K. Miller Jr., and Arleen R. Bessette. She has been on television and radio, appeared at the Denver Botanical Gardens, and has led many forays and mycology classes, doing cooking demonstrations. She taught classes at the Open University at Virginia Tech; lectured at a workshop in Thailand explaining collecting, recording, and preserving fungi; and has been the recorder at more than 200 fungus forays. She has also had a cooking column in a Blacksburg, Virginia newspaper and has received the Lifetime Achievement Award for Contributions to Amateur Mycology from the Texas Mycological Society. She lives in McCall, Idaho.

Until Orson K. Miller Jr.'s death in June 2006, the Millers worked extensively in North America, including Alaska, Canada, Puerto Rico, the Dominican Republic, Jamaica, and Belize, as well as in Europe, Australia, New Zealand, and parts of Asia. In addition, they joined a large group of scientists conducting studies of Great Smoky Mountain National Park. This entailed the study and recording of all living things found in the park, including mushrooms, plants, insects, and animals. Similar studies are being conducted in many parts of North America.